Researching Post-compulsory Education

Jill Jameson and Yvonne Hillier

BLOOMSBURY
NEW DELHI • LONDON • OXFORD • NEW YORK • SYDNEY

BLOOMSBURY INDIA
Bloomsbury Publishing India Pvt. Ltd
Second Floor, LSC Building No. 4, DDA Complex, Pocket C–6&7,
Vasant Kunj, New Delhi 110070

BLOOMSBURY and the Diana logo are
trademarks of Bloomsbury Publishing Plc

First published 2003

This edition is published with permission from Bloomsbury Publishing Plc.
50 Bedford Square, London WC1B3DP

British library Cataloguing-in-Publication Data
A catalogue record for this book is available from the British Library.

Library of Congress Cataloging-in-Publication Data
A catalogue record of this book has been applied for.

ISBN: 978-93-94701-16-8

Typeset by Photoprint, Torquay, Devon
Printed and bound in India by Replika Press Pvt. Ltd

Contents

Series Editor's Introduction

The *Continuum Research Methods* series aims to provide undergraduate, Masters and research students with accessible and authoritative guides to particular aspects of research methodology. Each title looks specifically at one topic and gives it in-depth treatment, very much in the tradition of the *Rediguide* series of the 1960s and 1970s.

Such an approach allows students to choose the books that are most appropriate to their own projects, whether they are working on a short dissertation, a medium-length work (15–40 000 words) or a fully-fledged thesis at MPhil or PhD level. Each title includes examples of students' work, clear explication of the principles and practices involved, and summaries of how best to check that your research is on course.

In due course, individual titles will be combined into larger books and, subsequently, into encyclopaedic works for reference.

The series will also be of use to researchers designing funded projects, and to supervisors who wish to recommend in-depth help to their research students.

Richard Andrews

Foreword

This is aimed at practitioners in post-compulsory education and training (PCET), in particular those in further education colleges (FE), who wish to carry out small-scale research on a change management project in the workplace. It can be used within post-compulsory education and training/further education (PCET/FE) institutions by senior and middle managers, teaching and support staff, and by researchers coming into PCET/FE from outside an institution. The work aims to provide seven basic principles for carrying out action research to improve the implementation of change in the three key areas of: technical, practical curriculum and organizational change.

Having jointly experienced many curriculum changes and organizational restructurings in adult, community, further and higher education, but never having yet seen a guidance manual dealing exclusively with helping staff carry out research to inform change management in PCET/FE, we felt that writing about it was long overdue. Since change is constant and inevitable, this small guidebook attempts to help people in the sector face the inevitability of change in positive, empowering ways fostering long-term survival and growth. We argue neither for change for its own sake, nor for resistance to change, but for collaborative, well-conducted processes of inquiry to inform action on planned changes.

We hope this work celebrates some existing considerable successes in researching the management of change in PCET/FE that colleagues and institutions have achieved. We also hope that it will help colleagues to avoid, in the future, some of the failures and problems that have occurred over the years, through lack of information, guidance and support in carrying out collaborative research to shape and drive planned changes. The guidance within the following pages aims to address that gap.

Acknowledgements

We wish to acknowledge the work of the Learning and Skills Development Agency (LSDA), and that of numerous practitioners across the UK in the Learning and Skills Research Network (LSRN) for many valuable insights, research papers and discussions that have formed the background to the production of this work on PCET/FE research. We thank our LSDA/LSRN colleagues Dr Andrew Morris, Dr Ursula Howard, the National LSRN Planning Group, and the London and South East LSRN for their help, support and inspiration over many years in developing the capacity of researchers in the Further Education and Learning and Skills sectors. We also thank our many colleagues, friends and institutions in the sector who have provided, over the years, exemplary classroom, technical and managerial models for coping with change.

Jill Jameson and Yvonne Hillier

Dedication

from Yvonne to John
from Jill to PHJ, MJLJ, Kevin, Imogen and Paul B.

1

Introduction

Growing research within the sector

> Research: careful search or inquiry, endeavour to discover facts by scientific study of a subject, course of critical investigation
>
> (*Concise OED*)

A few years ago in the mid 1990s, the Further Education Funding Council (FEFC) did not fund research, only programmes of learning. Yet at the same time, managers and staff in the further education sector were being asked to create mission statements, visions, identify their markets, specify their strengths and weaknesses and develop new and innovative ways to enable people to learn. How could these analyses take place without embarking on fact-finding exercises? The very process of asking questions about how many learners an institution had in any one year compared with another, or how many learners were achieving what kind of qualification in what kind of mode of programme delivery was one of conducting research. The sector did not always employ market researchers or academic researchers to undertake this kind of analysis – staff did it themselves.

Very few people would have labelled their work as research, often because the public idea of research is one where people wear white coats, carry clipboards and look intensely through bubbling liquids in strange scientific apparatus. Yet many people in further education institutions have been involved in research activities, sometimes without recognizing that this has been 'research' and will continue to be so. This book is aimed at practitioners from all sections within the further education field who wish to know more about how to ask questions about their work, find answers effectively, and implement solutions.

Summing up a diverse sector

We could sum up the diverse sector of post-compulsory education and training (PCET) as educational provision for post-compulsory age learners at sub-degree level in a range of post-16, adult and extramural education and training institutions. There is also a large amount of provision we could call 'post-compulsory' in higher education, especially in full and part-time extramural, adult and evening classes. The PCET sector educates the largest number of learners in the UK. The vast range of learners served by the sector includes around six million in post-16 education and training, funded by a Learning and Skills Council budget of more than £7 billion. The total number of learners in PCET in England and Wales is, however, far greater than this, if we add in the many other higher education, training, voluntary and community initiatives in PCET education and skills.

The diversity of this sector is its most complex and striking feature. To call it a distinct 'sector' is in itself quite a stretch of the imagination, as there are so many institutions, organizations, funding regimes, different kinds of learners, trainees, award-bearing courses and types of provision covered by the term 'post-compulsory education' that its diversity almost defies analysis. Using the term 'sector' as a shortcut to encompass this massive differentiation, though, we note that in the wide-ranging miscellany of PCET, several features stand out in common.

A patchy history of marginalization, under-funding, dilapidated premises, old equipment, poorly-funded learners and often overworked staff have sometimes been key factors causing particular demands for effective change in post-compulsory education. Being large, a bit rambling and very diverse, the sector has for years faced considerable challenges that have threatened to stretch its resources beyond capacity. Some institutions have performed outstandingly well in overcoming these difficulties by generating significant opportunities, growth and additional funding. Some of these have appropriately been given awards for being 'beacon' institutions, leading the way in a variety of innovative areas of activity.

In general, though, the sector suffers from under-funding, considering the large numbers of learners it serves. Vastly under-researched in comparison with the data potentially available to it, the strengths of the post-compulsory sector have sometimes been overlooked and its achievements undervalued. In the public imagination, different parts of the sector such as further education colleges and training organizations have sometimes either been comparatively invisible, or seen as under-performing. Our view is that post-compulsory education and training needs more recognition. This relative position may have resulted, in part, from a lack of funded time for legitimately subsidized research, reflection and publication by its practitioners. It is time to redress this.

A developing interest in research

It would be inaccurate to say that further education practitioners have not been involved in research in the past. The work of the Further Education Unit (FEU) in the 1980s involved a number of development projects that provided information about good practice in the sector which was then disseminated widely (FEU, 1992, 1994). These projects were undertaken by practitioners in further education institutions. Such development activities were supported by professional development for staff provided through the Further Education Staff College (FESC), which also offered all staff within the sector opportunities to examine their practice and develop knowledge and skills.

The Further Education Development Agency (FEDA), which resulted from the merger of the FEU and FESC, continued this development work throughout the 1990s. In 1996, a residential conference took place at the Staff College where practitioners were invited to discuss how research in further education was being conducted and if it should be fostered among a wider group of practitioners. A small group who attended this conference decided to continue the debate and so began the development of the further education research network (FERN), with its first annual conference in December, 1997. The creation of a research journal (*College Research*) in 1998 and the creation of regional networks followed shortly afterwards.

Today, FEDA has become the Learning and Skills Development Agency (LSDA). It supports an annual conference of the Learning and Skills Research Network (LSRN), regional summer conferences, and the re-titled *Learning and Skills Research Journal*. In addition, government funding was allocated to create the Learning and Skills Research Centre (LSRC, 2002) with a number of research aims, including building research capacity in the field.

The LSRC in particular will:

commission major studies;
enhance the impact of research on policy and practice;
help increase the overall research effort, build on existing knowledge from research and practice;
contribute to the development of capacity in post-16 research;
develop a wider range of research methods and engage in 'blue skies' studies (LSRC, 2002, p. 5).

In addition to the above research initiatives, we note the significant influence and valuable work of the Further Education Research Association (FERA), the *Journal of Research in post-compulsory Education*, the published works of a number of key academic experts, and much ongoing research linked to post-compulsory education by the Society for Research in Higher Education. Existing journals *Action Research*, the *Journal of Further and Higher Education*, *Studies in Continuing Education* and the new journal *Action Learning: Research and Practice* are all valuable contributors in this field. A number of important LSC-funded skills-based and marketing, business and community research projects have also contributed to the PCET research field significantly. There are, in addition, several ESRC (Economic and Social Research Council)-funded, ERDF (European Regional Development Fund)-funded, DfES (Department for Education and Science), and HEFCE (Higher Education Funding Council)-funded initiatives on research linked with or carried out within the post-compulsory sector. A wide range of research activities is therefore already in progress *with* the sector, and has been for some years, but we note that in most cases these initiatives are *based in universities or outside organizations*, rather than within further education institutions.

Continuing a trend

Within further education, there have been, and continue to be, numerous activities that require research approaches, particularly those that relate to market research, such as finding out what programmes potential learners would be interested in taking, or what barriers prevent learners from attending college programmes. In addition, there are many FE staff who decide to study for a higher degree, which involves undertaking a small research project. Many staff study for a research degree for which they need to sustain a substantial research undertaking in order to gain their qualification. Very few of the research theses are ever published or the results of the research disseminated among the wide audience that comprises the further education sector. Yet within these unpublished theses and research reports resides important, practical knowledge about how to improve learning activities, carry out change management projects, improve our knowledge of how to assess more effectively, or how to use new technologies.

Simultaneously, more and more information is becoming available through the world wide web. People are increasingly aware of other ways of teaching and learning by reading about different processes, by different practitioners from different sectors and different countries. So we have a situation where we can know far more about our professional practice through the use of electronic and more traditional means of communication. At the same time many of us are undertaking small-scale projects that never see the light of day. It is as though there are fireworks exploding all the time but we can never quite capture them.

Capacity building

Although there is much research going on in further education, there is still a difficulty that funding for research is given mainly to organizations outside of the sector, particularly higher education institutions. This means that research is more often *done to* rather than *done by* further education practitioners. Higher education academic staff are expected to be experienced research practitioners, who research into their specialist fields and who seek and obtain funds to achieve this aim. Research funding bodies expect that staff who bid for funds are supported to undertake this research by their institutions. This has resulted in a situation where further education institutions are not yet seen to be capable of supporting the kind of research that research funding bodies are prepared to fund. However, private research bodies and research and development organizations may well be interested in working with individuals within the further education sector, and there are many examples of such collaborations (Morris, 2002).

We need, therefore, to develop the capacity to undertake research among individuals and institutions in the further education sector. We need to demonstrate that we have practitioners who know their subject specialism *and* know how to research it. This does not mean that we have to become researchers conducting 'blue skies' research, the kind of research that tackles enduring problems of humankind, or develops new machines. We *do* need to be able to respond to the increasing demands for knowledge about our field. Many people begin working in further education having worked in a particular industry or sector. They are highly experienced in their field. They now have to gain a teaching qualification based on the Further Education National Training Organization standards (FENTO), part of which expects them to continually develop their professional practice.

For example, staff in the sector must:

Identify developments in vocational and educational fields relevant to their own areas of work and to FE in general (G2a).
Consider the relevance of current developments to their own practice within existing and potential roles (G2b).
Monitor curriculum developments in their own subject and keep up-to-date with new topics and new areas of work (G2c).
Consider and implement appropriate changes in programme design and delivery that best reflect current vocational and educational developments (G2e).
Explore ways of encouraging learners to work effectively on their own (H1a) (FENTO, 1999).

Since people are not expected to be experienced teachers before they work in the further education sector, we cannot have any expectations that people are experienced researchers. However many programmes delivered in the sector require that learners undertake a small investigation into an aspect of their curriculum, or practice. How can we support learners to do this unless we, too, have experience of small-scale investigation, project management and identifying appropriate research questions?

So we need to develop our research skills to help learners develop their own research skills, to help us advance our own professional practice. We need to evolve this practice so that it is based on sound evidence rather than unchallenged assumptions. We also need to enable institutions to respond to calls for evidence and research into the extremely varied programme areas, institutional services and managerial activities that comprise the further education sector.

There are opportunities for FE staff to undertake investigations through the Research into Quality and Achievement (RQA) initiative, linked with the LSDA and funded by the DfES (RQA, 2002). Here, research projects aim to identify improvements in quality and achievement within the sector. These are small development projects that specifically aim to make a difference.

A growing capacity for research in the new Learning and Skills sector is, on the positive side, now informing a new dynamic opportunity for funded research to inform and guide the sector. Influential major research studies more recently carried out, such as work by Martinez and Munday (1998) and Bloomer and Hodkinson (1997), have begun to shape a new agenda. The growing capability of the LSRN is spurring new growth and interest nationally in research, while the Learning and Skills Research Centre is for the first time giving practitioners an opportunity to gain funds for major new research into post-compulsory education and training.

Policy issues

Both the current government, and its predecessor, have called for evidence-based policy-making to ensure that decisions draw upon reliable information, rather than upon ideas that have no basis in reality. There are some important government policies which affect the way in which the Learning and Skills Sector operates. Further education comprises a large part of the learning and skills sector and therefore evidence-based policy increasingly affects further education.

Perhaps the most important policies in 2003 are those that help meet the government drive to expand higher education announced at the 1997 Labour Party Conference and later refined by ministers into the pledge that by 2010, 50 per cent of young people under 30 will have experienced higher education (Russell, 2001). The reason that this affects further education is that a large proportion of these potential additional learners are likely to be taught in further education rather than higher education institutions. Already a significant percentage of all further education activity is at the higher education level. If we are to make some changes to attract new learners into the colleges, do we know how best to go about it?

This can be turned into numerous research questions, as follows.

Factual research questions

The first set could ask questions of fact, for example:

What proportion of young people aged under 30 are there locally, regionally and nationally?
How many are already in further and higher education?

Speculative and process-based questions

The second type of questions are more speculative, and ask about process, or are based on speculation. These include:

How many learners can be encouraged to gain qualifications that would enable them to progress to higher education?

Are there particular ways of teaching that attract people who traditionally have not participated in higher education?
Is there evidence that foundation degrees attract and retain people who have not traditionally participated in higher education?

Organizational and systems-based questions

We can also ask questions about institutions, too. For example, there are policies about collaborating between sectors in regional partnerships, such as in the New Technology Institutes, Partnerships for Progression and Lifelong Learning Partnerships. We might want to know:

What systems of collaboration work most effectively?
How can progression be fostered?
How are learner records used to inform future learning activities?

Assessment and accreditation questions

You may have read in the press every year, when the GCSE and A level results are released, that standards are slipping, or that we are 'dumbing down'. There is a growing demand for new forms of qualifications, and even that GCSEs and A levels should now be abandoned in favour of a baccalaureate-style qualification. Again, we can begin to ask research questions about the way in which learning is assessed and accredited:

Is there evidence that a particular style of assessment privileges one group of people over another?
How can we identify ways to encourage disaffected

young people to continue to learn, in the workplace or in colleges after the compulsory leaving age?

Is there evidence that a baccalaureate is more effective at fostering learning than the two-stage GCSE/A level scheme?

What evidence, if any, is there that the Scottish system of highers attracts more learners?

Government and local policy implementation questions

There are other government policies that relate less to learning as such, but make the assumption that learning enables progression to employment, or fosters citizenship, or participation in community life. For example, job seekers are asked to take part in initiatives such as the New Deal, or Modern Apprenticeships, and refugees and asylum seekers have numerous procedures to go through in order to remain within the UK. They may not be entitled to work but are entitled to training or to learn English. There is an increasing policy drive to ensure that people with mental health difficulties can participate fully within society, and the government paper 'Valuing People' provides immense scope to achieve these aims. Our research questions concerning these wider reaching policies could include:

What steps can be taken to enable people with mental health difficulties to engage in society?

What is the role of further education institutions in enabling people with mental health difficulties to develop autonomy and independence?

What role can be played by advice and guidance staff in helping unemployed people gain the necessary skills and knowledge to gain employment, perhaps in new sectors?

What can labour-force surveys and labour-market information tell us about the skills and knowledge required to plug gaps in areas of skills shortages?

European legislative, policy initiative and wider international questions

Finally, we can look further afield to European legislation and policy initiatives. Many of these reflect the interests of any nation state, but perhaps the most important policies relate to lifelong learning, including upskilling of the workforce, and enabling people to use new technologies and have access to these. An OECD (Organization for Economic Co-operation and Development) report on lifelong learning has helped identify good practice in meeting some of these aims, but also provides survey information about how far away we are in providing funds, programmes and sharing knowledge so that lifelong learning becomes an integral part of our lives throughout Europe (OECD, 2000, 2001). We can also focus our research on examining a range of wider international issues in learning and teaching.

This may seem a long way from what we may be doing with a group of learners on a Monday afternoon, or when we work in the learning resources centre, or enrol new learners. If you are a manager, you may be more aware of some of the government initiatives and policies, but often people are so busy implementing awarding body regulations, institutional quality assurance requirements, health and safety requirements and meeting inspection deadlines, that there is little time to stand back and ask questions about how we go about our business and identify if we could do things differently.

Yet, without this important time to think, question and challenge, we are in danger of moving forward with ill-defined practices, not underpinned by research and theory, and not leading to an openness to try out new ideas. We can not expect to create massive research projects within the limits of our everyday work, but we can begin to make a difference if we take stock of the many changes that we are being asked to introduce. We can also begin to search for evidence on how best to implement them, evaluate their impact and identify for ourselves the questions that would improve the main focus of what we do, which is ultimately to enable people to learn.

Small-scale research

The kind of research that can be undertaken by an individual tutor, manager or team is usually bounded by constraints, lack of funding, lack of time, physical location and the kinds of opportunities that exist to engage with people in other parts of the institution or from outside. The scale of any research undertaking, therefore, is comparatively small. Indeed, the title of such research is 'small-scale research'. What does this mean?

You may have been asked to participate in surveys conducted by market research organizations. You may have been asked to answer a series of questions while walking down the street, or may have received a questionnaire through the post. You would have been part of a large-scale survey, where hundreds and possibly thousands of people respond to questionnaires. To conduct such a survey requires vast resources. You need people to create the questionnaire, produce and distribute multiple copies, collate the responses and analyse the data. By contrast, in a small-scale research project, you could ask a group of learners in one course to respond to a questionnaire that you have created. Clearly, the latter example is on a much smaller scale.

You could also conduct interviews with the same small

group of people, or you could decide to analyse the results of examination scores for that particular course over the past five years. All of these research processes are small in scale. So 'small-scale research' is simply that which does not involve large numbers of people, different sites, and does not require the analysis of vast quantities of data gathered from the research process.

Case studies

Perhaps the most appropriate way of conducting small-scale research is to consider your project as a case study. Case studies originated from the examination of professional conduct, for example in legal practice. Here, decisions are made on the basis of examples tried in the judiciary. Law is interpreted as a result of these cases. In further education institutions, many specialist professional areas of knowledge exist, in which improvements in practice from case studies can be developed. These areas of subject specialism are often very different from each other in different colleges, a trend now particularly recognized and encouraged in the Centres of Vocational Excellence (CoVE) initiative of the Learning and Skills Council.

How can we know that a particular practice, which is found to be successful in one subject discipline, or centre will easily transfer to a completely different subject discipline, geographical location or college with a completely different demographic profile? The answer is that we cannot assume that what is discovered in one place will happen in another. This is where we can only make what Michael Bassey calls 'fuzzy generalisations' (Bassey, 1999, p. 12). In other words, we know, as a result of our small-scale research into our particular example or case, that a certain phenomenon is occurring, but we can only generalize from this example to a wider context in a hazy, or fuzzy way.

Sceptics at this stage may be asking why bother to conduct small-scale research if you cannot use the results in a wider application? However, the main issue for all educational research is that we are dealing with people. We have as many individual ways of looking at the world as we have people in it. We cannot devise standard laws that predict, describe and explain human behaviour in the same way that we can state that heating water to one hundred degrees centigrade at sea level will result in boiling. I am sure that many managers would be delighted to find a way of predicting that if they take one course of action, there will be one consequence!

Such easy solutions to the problems of human behaviour are, however, simply not feasible in a real world populated by diverse, complex human individuals. We therefore need a way of researching people's activities in further education that simultaneously (a) embraces complexity and (b) allows us to apply sound results from useful, realistic, time-limited research in busy colleges with very overworked staff who have little or no time for research and (c) who have often not previously rated research very highly as an activity anyhow! We need to recognize the importance and reality of the pressures facing organizations, staff and learners, but still lead people gently to an awareness that, far from being a waste of time, a well-conducted action research process can be enjoyable, empowering and can, in the end, save people large amounts of time through the improvements it enables.

There are many different approaches to case study in educational research that can potentially satisfy these demands, and that may appeal to even the most research-sceptical staff. These can be summarized into three main categories:

those that seek to implement a change;
those that evaluate;
those that develop a theory of the educational practice (see Stenhouse, 1975).

What are the benefits of undertaking case studies as small-scale research?

By focusing on a particular issue, or group of people, or event, we limit the number of factors that may affect the outcome of our enquiry. For example, suppose we want to know if a new online learning resource helps our learners on a maths A level course. We want to know if we can improve their grades, in a programme where traditionally they have not achieved against the national benchmark. We may find that there is an increase in the first module results, but that this tails off by the end of the course. By focusing on one aspect of a maths course, we deliberately limit our investigation and ignore the influences on the different types of learner that we could be working with, the different disciplines and the different college facilities. This means accepting that we will not find out whether online learning resources in another subject, such as electronics, will have the same effect. However, this does not matter if we are only concerned with teaching maths A level learners and we want to improve their grades. Our findings may be of interest to people throughout the college who are all implementing online learning with their learners, but it is up to them to try out a research study to find out what is happening there. Of course, we may wish to undertake further research as a result of our first case study, to test out whether our results are upheld in the different subject disciplines, or with mature learners and so forth. Our first case study, then, can act as a 'pilot' or test of a phenomenon that we wish to investigate. It is manageable, and can provide stepping stones to further practices. Our case study also provides evidence more quickly because we are focusing only on a small group of learners, and on one particular subject.

To challenge certainties is to 'see new'

When we do undertake more case study research, we are in a position to make what Stake calls assertions (Stake, 1994), which are more than the 'petites generalisations' that can be made on the basis of a single case study, and help us move towards 'grandes generalisations'. Assertions are made about a wider population and, in research terms, provide a firmer foundation on which to base our theories about what we do. They also provide more evidence upon which we can test our theories.

Case studies therefore have the advantage that they are manageable. Because they 'drill down' into a small piece of ground, they also provide important information, in exactly the same way that drilling for oil does. They help us deal with the complexity of any situation, recognizing that we cannot know all that there is to know about every event. Simons eloquently argues that:

> living with paradox is crucial to understanding. The tension between the study of the unique and the need to generalize is necessary to reveal both the *unique* and the *universal* and the *unity* of that understanding. To live with ambiguity, to challenge certainty, to creatively encounter, is to arrive, eventually at 'seeing' new.
>
> (Simons, 1996, p. 238)

Making a difference through research

If we now return to the idea that we can undertake research to make a difference, we can now draw together the three strands of undertaking research in further education as noted earlier. Here, our argument is that further education is a sector that is immensely complex, is required to implement change resulting from government policy and initiatives and, at the same time, needs to investigate its own practices.

It also happens to be a sector on which vast quantities of data are held. We know about learners' previous qualifications, where they live, what programmes they are taking, and how well their achievements match those across the sector as a whole. We also know about staff who work in the sector, their qualifications, where they live and work, and how well their practices measure up to national benchmarks for learners and for a variety of quality assurance processes. We have data on participation rates within geographical locations, employment rates, success rates. We even have information about our practices and their effectiveness residing in project reports and theses sitting on shelves in colleges, homes and higher education institutions.

We know that we need more evidence to help us influence national, regional and local policy-making, and to provide evidence on how successful current policy initiatives are. If we are going to influence future decision-making and gain control of how our sector is funded, managed and developed, then we need to ensure that we are capable of undertaking the necessary research to provide the evidence.

Finally, we can make a difference by starting in a small way, through the use of research into individual practices and by using our evidence to further test out ideas in other situations. Through the approach of critical reflection on what we do, and by being open to investigating new ideas, we can, and will, make a difference. The next step is to equip ourselves to undertake the research and, in particular, to undertake action research, where we are implementing change.

Action research

Case studies primarily focused on implementing change immediately become entwined with another research term, 'action research'. Here, the idea is that people do not simply look at what is happening in a descriptive way. They are not trying to make a difference to what they are doing, but investigate the effects of what they are doing as they do it. We feel that small scale action research is particularly useful as a method for PCET in general and for the FE sector in particular, in view of the lack of funds and time generally available for research.

Action research, by its very name, implies doing something. As noted above, research can involve looking backwards to things that have already happened and evaluate their effectiveness. Action research is something that investigates what is happening now. It has a clear aim of making a difference as it takes place. As Kemmis and McTaggart note, action research is not something that is done to people, it is 'research by particular people on their own work, to help them improve what they do' (Kemmis and McTaggart, 1992, p. 21).

In order for action research to be successful, individuals must be critical in the sense of being able to stand back and critique their own and colleagues' practices. They must be prepared to participate in questioning practices, and for the results of such research to be made public, providing accountability. Action research requires an ability to continually reflect, challenge and implement change.

The collaborative nature of action research is important. If I decide to introduce a new induction for learners into the programme area, I cannot do this all by myself. My colleagues must participate. Now with action research, this does not simply mean that they all use the new induction process with their learners. They need to observe what happens during the new process, to discuss with each other how this process is working, monitor and judge what is working and what is not, and to agree any changes that will be made. It is an iterative process, unlike one in which a change is introduced, monitored and evaluated at the end of a particular time scale. Action research is therefore *interventionist* in nature.

Action research is also something that can work on a small scale, where even one person can begin to reflect on and challenge current practices, and begin to create questions that could be answered through dialogue and action with colleagues. Action research is therefore deliberately challenging, but also emancipatory, because it releases people from the status quo and helps them take control over future practice. Yet the process is one of transparency, as it relies on dialogue, testing out ideas, and evaluating these.

Reflective practice

First, then, action research begins with posing a question, or identifying a problem. The link with reflective practice here is important. Some problems are presented to us as a result of being asked to introduce new ways of doing things, working with different groups of learners, or using new technologies for our learning resources. Here, we have no choice but to find a way to work effectively.

The way in which reflective practice can help action research is that we can begin to pose questions about our *current* ways of working, even if we have not got a 'problem' as such. In this way, we are not using research only to think of problems in almost a pathological sense (Kemmis and McTaggart, 1992), but rather as a tool to help us improve what we do, and to study the effects of what we do.

There are numerous rationales for using action research that are summarized well in the research literature by Cohen *et al.* (2000). Amongst these are the benefit of involving practitioners as part of the research, of empowering people to make a difference in their working lives, and adopting a more democratic process of research. However, creating a rationale for action research does not help us know how to do action research. What are the basic approaches to this form of research?

Action research procedures

Action research derives from the work of Kurt Lewin (1948) and has been particularly developed in the field of education by Lawrence Stenhouse (1975) and John Elliot (1991). However, most of this work has focused on educational research in schools. The principles are the same, whatever the context. The process can be summarized as follows.

The ten-step process

1. Identify the issue and decide that some kind of improvement or change is required.
2. Decide on what can be done, and what cannot be attempted. This relates particularly to Lewin's (1948)

ideas of force-field analysis, where there are some things that are within an individual's ability to change and others that are simply unmoveable. The idea is to find ways around the stumbling blocks, rather than to give up in despair. The area to be investigated, and the scale of this investigation is known as the field of action.

3. Decide on a general plan of action for the work that is to be done.
4. Break this plan of action down into specific steps.
5. Begin the action, but monitor every step along the way.
6. Monitoring the action requires 'fact finding' and being aware of unintended consequences of the action.
7. Revise the general plan in light of feedback from monitoring the first step.
8. Continue to take steps towards the goal of the action plan, revising according to the monitoring of the outcome of previous steps.
9. Keep a careful record of each decision made.
10. Evaluate the process at the end of the timescale, using the research data that has been gathered along the way.

The main difference between this form of research and other processes of implementing change is that there is a conscious effort to find information along the way with the express intention of making changes to the process as it happens. This is in contrast to waiting until the end of the evaluation period to identify the effects of a particular activity or initiative. The benefit of such a process is that change can be continually refined and it should help prevent a situation where people say, 'if only we had done x earlier, y would not have happened with its unfortunate consequences'.

The process cannot take place in a vacuum and it relies on collaboration between the actors in the field. In reality, the process is not so straightforward. As you will know from your own experience of working in a complex, dynamic environment, one form of change is not implemented exclusively. It invariably sits alongside other initiatives and monitoring how one change is affecting a situation is therefore not easy. The effects cannot be attributed solely to the change being implemented.

Let us return to the ten-step process. The first stage, identifying an issue, may be something done by an individual, members of a team or even a department or faculty. To be truly collaborative, it is important that all members are given the opportunity to identify the nature of the issue, define the problem and the course of action that will be taken.

The second and third stages require sketching out fully the plan of action. Again, the idea of action research means that monitoring is built into this process. Therefore, not only does this stage require careful decision-making about what steps are required, it also needs careful decision-making about what sort of information is necessary to inform decisions about how future steps will be taken.

Let us look at an example here, to illustrate what we mean. Suppose we want to introduce a new scheme of personal tutorials to encourage our learners to attend punctually and regularly in a college that has had poor achievement rates for mathematics. Our issue, then, is one of improving learning and achievement rates by improving attendance and punctuality. Our field of action is an A level course in maths. We have a team of two full-time and four hourly-paid lecturers responsible for 50 learners, all of them aged between 18 and 20.

To ensure that we have defined our issue carefully, we will want to look at what has already been done elsewhere. This may involve talking to colleagues from other departments in our college, researching the literature written on achievement and retention, supporting learners and using a tutorial system. As a result of our preliminary 'fact finding' we may want to make changes to our original idea. However, let us assume that we still believe that introducing a scheme to record attendance and punctuality may drive up achievement rates. This is our hypothesis, or hunch. It is this hypothesis that our action research will set out to test, by taking action and researching into the effects of this action.

Our plan of action is to introduce a personal tutorial system where each learner has to have a regular half-hour tutorial each week. There will be a record system of attendance and punctuality that will be available for inspection by tutors and learners on the new intranet for the department. This has all the necessary security systems to ensure that only the learners and tutors for this course have access to this data.

The specific action plan involves allocating learners to tutors, creating a timetable for the tutorials, introducing the record-keeping system of learners logging on when they arrive, and when they leave the sessions. It will also involve creating a series of key issues to be covered in the tutorials, including discussion of attendance and punctuality, and identifying where action needs to be taken to encourage learners to attend regularly.

How will we know that the first step, introducing a record-keeping system, will work? What data do we need to collect? Who is going to do this? We also need to know whether our tutorial system is effective. Again, what data do we need to inform us about this? How often should we collect evidence, and what constitutes evidence of effectiveness?

These questions are the sort that the whole team must be involved in posing and finding solutions to. It is no good introducing an action research project, perhaps as a result of the course director being told to improve achievement rates by senior management, without ensuring that the course team is both engaged in, and able to work collaboratively on, the research project. In other words, the team has to have a shared vision of what the problem is, what action is agreed and how this will be carried out.

Our next three stages, implementing a step, monitoring it, and evaluating and refining our planned stages, involve further collaborative work. We may decide to introduce team meetings on a fortnightly basis to discuss how our record system is working. We may already meet on this basis, but need to include an additional agenda item. We may decide that part of our evidence-gathering involves team members keeping diaries of their interactions with learners. We could decide to use the intranet, particularly for an online discussion of issues arising from our interactions with our learners. These discussions can be archived, and will provide an important record of our deliberations and how we make changes to our original plan.

Part of our analysis may include interviews with learners and other course tutors with whom they interact. There may be spin-offs for other subjects that the learners are studying. Our intervention may have improved their general attendance, or it may have worsened it. We need to know the effects that our intervention is having on the rest of their time in college (or out of it!).

By now, some of you will be deciding that action research is too time-consuming and definitely not possible to use. However, decisions about how much information you gather, how often and for what purpose, is dependent upon the time constraints that you have. Part of your reflection on the process will include reflecting on the way the methodology you have chosen is implemented. The joy of action research is that it enables you to be aware of, and ready to take action about, the change you are implementing, the way you are doing so, and the way in which you are researching the change.

There are difficulties in using this method. For example, most colleges have a hierarchical system, where line managers have responsibility and power to implement change. In collaborative research, all participants have equal voice. Yet this may be hard to achieve when one of the team members is a line manager. A further difficulty is how the action research is reported and who such a report is for. Suppose, in our example, the course manager wants to write a report to the Board of Governors. Who owns the report? How will it be used? Does the report have to be written in 'academic' jargon and, if not, will it be given status and credence?

Finally, there will always be resistance to any change, and nods of 'I told you so' when things do not go according to plan. It takes an assertive person to be able to continue on a reflective and active path to implement change. That said, action research has the benefit of using a carefully constructed cycle of issue identification, planning, implementing, monitoring and evaluating. It draws upon and reinforces reflective practice, adopts a critical stance, can be emancipatory and enables professional development of participants. It provides practitioners with the opportunity to undertake research and make a difference.

Building communities of practice in post-compulsory and FE research

To really make a difference in a wider sense, we also need to link our research into a community of practice. We have witnessed that the development of the regional Learning and Skills Research Networks (LSRN's) across the UK during the period 1996–2002 has provided an example of the effective building of useful communities of practice in post-compulsory education research. These comprise many education research participants from further, higher and training organizations throughout the UK.

The key point about a community of educational practice is that it is a voluntary, organic network of professionals engaged in debate on key issues with a sense of commitment, vitality, spontaneity and shared concern that cannot be prescribed or enforced (Wenger *et al.*, 2002). From such a network of interested voluntary participants, real learning and capacity-building in research techniques can come.

Wenger *et al.* (2002) identify useful principles to stimulate the effective operation of communities of practice. They advise such communities to plan for organic growth, enabling dialogue at a variety of participation levels including both 'private and community spaces' with practitioners within and outside the group. A useful focus on 'value' combining both 'familiarity and excitement' and developing a 'rhythm for the community' should be planned for communities of practice.

In the development of the Learning and Skills Development Agency (LSDA) Research Networks (LSRNs) across the UK in 1995–2002, organizing a routine national annual conference, local summer conferences, and regular local LSRN meetings has set in motion the kind of rhythm for national and local events that Wenger *et al.* (2002) advocate. A rich combination of professional and social networking at these regular events has, over several years, created a momentum stimulating the growth of further research and networking activities.

Building our own community of practice within our

college, or linking into an existing neighbouring community of practice, is a way of developing practitioner knowledge and research effectively. By connecting to research networks such as the regional LSRN's, your own local network can enrich its activities and develop useful contacts to inform and update practitioners on research methodologies, and to grow further work. Fund-raising, bid-writing and staff development opportunities for PCET/FE practitioner research available through the ESRC, Learning and Skills Research Centre and the LSDA itself are regularly advertised through these networks.

The focus for our own local community of practice depends, of course, on the nature of the research questions that interest us, the geographical area we work in, and/or the kind of change management project we are planning. College chief executives, PCET/FE senior managers, curriculum and marketing managers, for example, might wish to create their own research interest groups to examine questions particularly relevant to the areas of activity they manage. Teacher-practitioners or trainers, by contrast, may be specifically focused on curriculum issues relating to classroom practice in a particular subject. People more interested in the technical aspects of using research for change, such as IT, learning resources, library and distance learning practitioners, on the other hand, may have specialist local and national networks of their own that they feel are more appropriate for building a community of practice.

We have noted that there is a developing interest in the growth and importance of research to the PCET/FE sector. In discussing this, we observed that a number of national initiatives developed in recent years are contributing proactively to the development of research capacity in the sector. Outlining the need for the capacity building of research in further education in particular, we noted the continuing difficulty of a lack of funding for, and recognition of, research.

We therefore argue that this has resulted in a situation in which the FE sector has more often been the *object* of research studies than the producer of research output and publications. In spite of this, FE staff still need to carry forward a number of initiatives that are research-related. This trend is increasing rather than reducing, and has particular importance in respect of the implementation of the FENTO standards, and the implementation of a number of key government, curricular and European policy initiatives including the expansion of higher education.

Affirming the importance of practitioners having time and resources to reflect on their work, we have argued for a link between case study research on individual practice and action research, in which practitioners aim to make a difference to improve practice through research in action. We outlined the key procedures for action research, including a ten-step process, in which we identify an issue and develop research according to a plan that is monitored and revised as we proceed. We noted the significant role of action research in planning, implementing and evaluating change effectively.

The following section of our book will now provide more specific details of different types of action research for change. It will then focus on seven key principles for implementing effective practitioner action research for managing change.

2

Overview of Small-scale Research Evaluation of Change Management

Heraclitus said, around 500 BC, that we could not step into the same river twice, for 'other and yet other waters are always flowing on'. If this Greek philosopher's premise was in some ways correct – and our common sense experience seems to agree with it – that everything is always changing, then people, settings and institutions are always permanently fluid. We are always changing from our present state, sometimes for better, sometimes for worse. And so it is in the post-compulsory education sector – the most permanent feature of which is that change is constant. If change is constant and inevitable, then flowing with it in a skilful, intelligent way, controlling those aspects under our control, and accepting aspects that are not, is perhaps the most useful approach, enabling us to benefit, adapt and survive in a healthy, advantageous way.

We noted in the first section that key government-driven initiatives setting targets for change have strongly emerged in the past several years. These have put pressure on PCET institutions, particularly those in adult, community and further education, to meet ever-harder targets. These encompass improvements in the quality of teaching and learning, learner achievement and retention, and budgetary accountability. Forced by the need to drive down costs and improve both performance and accountability, many ACE, sixth form and FE colleges have responded by restructuring their staffing, anticipating that these changes will bring about improvements in delivery and performance. Although the links between planned changes and measurable resulting improvements have rarely been tested thoroughly, enforced plans for changes in delivery methods still proceed with regular, unquestioned certainty that from such and such particular intentions, such and such specific results will follow.

Life is often not so easily predictable. Inadequately implemented change projects and under-researched curriculum and managerial experimentation routinely result in patchy successes at best. Only around one third of major change initiatives, even when well resourced in the most suitable circumstances, are effective. The high cost of imperfectly implemented educational changes can result not only in financial loss, but also in longer-term damage to staff morale, curriculum delivery and learner achievement.

It is important to build research capacity to address the gap between the intentions behind planned changes and their results. Clear guidelines for this are particularly useful. These can help us not only to 'mind the gap', in observing the difference between intention and reality. They can also assist substantially to close up that gap, so that we are much more effective in our actions, as the basic sketches in Figure 2.1 and 2.2 illustrate.

The value of action research as real-life study in the management of change

The management of change can usefully involve a collaborative application of action research techniques. This application of action research links with the concept of

Intentions behind change	Gap	Results of change

Figure 2.1 Intentions behind changes in FE are not always fulfilled in the results.

Intentions behind change	Research in action finds solutions and reduces gap	Results of change

Figure 2.2 We can address the gap between intention and results through research in action.

'emancipatory action research' in challenging the operation of existing systems, hierarchical and social groups. It aims to understand and improve the operation of organizations and systems by introducing changes in democratic, participative ways. The work of Argyris and Schön (1974) on 'double-loop learning' that questions and challenges organizational value systems, Shön (1987) on 'reflection-in-action' and that of Zuber-Skerritt (1996) on action research for organizational change are key texts here.

The main value of action research as real-life study becomes visible in the process of useful application to a given problem, or desired new solution, posed by potential real world change. Many problems desperately need such solutions, if the good intentions behind change programmes are to be linked with improved results.

Sometimes we need to focus on solutions that are working already and learn to disseminate these to improve other areas of operation. As Robson (1993) observes 'systematic enquiry is a useful potential tool for those seeking improvement' (p. 431).

Our approach to this is one based on an evolutionary process in which small-scale local action research proceeds iteratively through a number of stages, adapted to the specific local situation. We describe below an action research change model for pilot-testing our organizational readiness to carry out a change process in education and/or a more limited gradual renewal. In discussing this model, we suggest we should check whether our resources, staff/learner capacity and commitment to change are positioned for the implementation process to be more, rather than less, effective. We suggest an initial pilot is needed to assess first of all whether we are ready for change, for gradual renewal, or need to re-examine the situation.

If this test is successful, we propose the pilot is followed by a main stage of implementing action research, as illustrated in Figure 2.3. For this we outline seven key principles later in this section. We will now discuss how to carry out a pilot test.

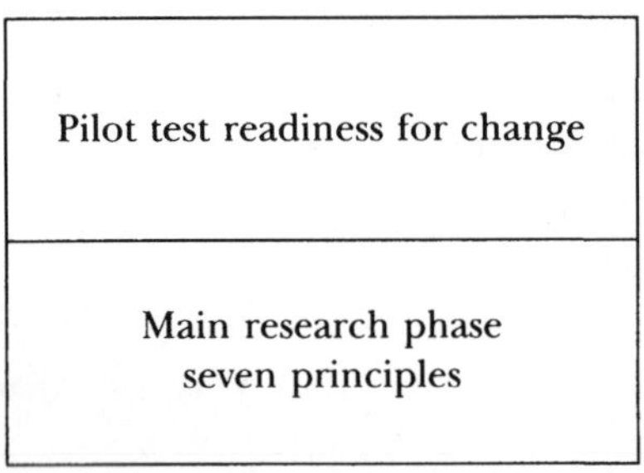

Figure 2.3 Model for small scale change management research in action.

Pilot research to test whether to proceed with major change or gradual renewal

When considering changes, it's useful to do some pilot research at the very outset to assess overall the likelihood of success for any planned changes. We assume that there is, in the first place, a set of issues, or one key issue, that comprise(s) the main reasons behind our need for suggested changes. This could be a problem with learning and teaching, one with retention and achievement, a need to introduce new curriculum initiatives, or a need for a new staffing structure. Or, it could be that we are impressed with the results of a particular area and want to disseminate good practice to other areas. In carrying out this initial pilot research, the concepts in the following section are key.

Basic guide to test whether to proceed with research-in-action change or renewal

How do we get started on deciding whether or not to proceed with any change process? One way is to follow a careful process of testing and questioning. We have called this the AMBER action research for change pilot model (see Figure 2.4). This involves the following:

1. **A**ssess key issue(s) of interest against organizational readiness for, and need for, change.
2. **M**ake time to reflect, consult, learn lessons from the literature of successful changes.
3. **B**uild a theory-based plan for research in action to achieve successful change.
4. **E**valuate changes previously carried out, check and modify plan against evaluation.

5. Research staff/learner views.

then use the results of 1–5 in deciding to 'STOP' or 'GO' with our plan.

This model for change is a practical outline of some initial tests we can undertake when major changes of a technical, curricular or organizational nature are being considered. We have called it an 'AMBER' research model, using a traffic light metaphor, to suggest a pause for reflection, consultation, planning and analysis, before we proceed either to 'STOP' or to 'GO' with our plans for change. It may be the case that we need to modify our plan and can achieve the same or better results through a process of evolutionary renewal, or a different kind of change. The model suggests we should check whether our resources, staff/learner capacity and commitment to change are positioned in such a way for the implementation process to prove more, rather than less, beneficial to the situation we want to change. We need to remember that performance improvements can be achieved through means other than drastic change, and sometimes change is in fact positively **not** what is needed!

A college principal who wants to improve the performance of her/his organization and staff may be able to achieve this effectively through gradual evolutionary renewal and skilful introduction of staff development initiatives, such as line management training, Investors' in People (IiP) and performance appraisal schemes. Focusing attention on the needs of staff may prove more effective in the long run than arousing the potential fear and hostility of the whole staff through restructuring schemes. There are many ways of achieving improvements less drastic to staff morale than whole organization restructuring. As Curtis (1994) notes, 'By being constantly aware of the need to change objectives, and in fact encouraging people to do so, an organization can

A	**Assess** key issues of concern vs organizational readiness and need for change	
M	**Make time** to reflect, consult, learn lessons from the literature of successful change	
B	**Build a theory-based plan** for our action research to achieve successful change	
E	**Evaluate** the implementation of previous changes: check and modify our plan against the evaluation	
R	**Research staff/learner views**	
	use the results of all the above to decide:	
	STOP this particular plan for change: modify the plan or focus on other ways to renew the situation and address key issues of concern	**GO** proceed with the next phase of our planned project in a focused change programme linked to action research

Figure 2.4 AMBER action research for change pilot model.

undergo continuous renewal and cushion the need for drastic change' (Curtis, 1994, p. 175).

Points to bear in mind when applying the AMBER model – some do's and don't's

In applying this model, some points to bear in mind when researching planned changes for performance improvements are as follows.

Do

tailor research to distinguish between *change* and *gradual renewal*;
plan research outcomes to *fix* problems, not *change problems*;
focus research on *solutions* as well as problems;
ensure time, resources and staff are available to carry out the research;
respect values, beliefs and cultural norms of staff and students when doing research;
buy ourselves additional time, if this is likely to be required, at the outset if possible;
ensure our plan is adaptable and flexible in responding to changing local circumstances.

Don't

rush into poorly executed programmes of action research under pressure from others;
focus only on the research process itself: focus on *what we want to achieve from it*;
focus on just the current situation, but also on ongoing changes and on the future;
forget to scrutinize our own assumptions, habits and prejudices.

Test its validity and reliability – some do's and don't's

(See also Section 9 for more detail on validity and reliability in evaluation of research.)

Do

test assumptions rigorously through multiple means;
ask for open and honest feedback from internal colleagues and outside experts;

link research objectives directly to the measurement of achieved outcomes;
determine reliable performance indicators for achieved outcomes (e.g. exam results);
use reliable methods to check if our research is valid;
use key informants to critique the draft and final research reports.

Don't

neglect to make checks for validity and reliability;
forget that there are many experts who can help in this area.

Practical teaching example

A lecturer who wants to improve student learning and attainment can achieve this in more than one way. Checking on learner views, and renewing delivery methods gradually in line with these, the lecturer can add to the learners' sense of involvement in the class and empowerment and avoid destabilizing their existing sense of continuity and well being.

Numerous managerial curriculum-focused initiatives have been introduced into colleges in the last few years. These include substantial reforms to the content and delivery of teaching, such as in curriculum 2000, key skills, new initiatives in work-based learning, competence-based qualifications, problem-based learning, information learning technology, widening participation and retention initiatives. Members of staff have often barely had time to adjust programmes according to one set of regulations when another new procedure is introduced. PCET staff have therefore often felt as though they were constantly changing the way they work without having the opportunity to find out if their methods have been effective. Almost all FE colleges have been engaged in restructurings to some degree during the past decade, and we need to be sensitive to the ways in which these processes have affected staff.

Practical curriculum management example

A curriculum manager who wants to bring in new timetabling or curriculum methods can research the background and knowledge-base for these changes, surveying the views of heads of department, lecturers, learners and other interested parties. The manager can then consider whether a process of gradual shared renewal of timetabling and curriculum methods could be more helpful than imposing major changes.

Respect for educational culture

The professionalism of teachers needs to be respected in both higher and further education. Recommendations for change should acknowledge, in the first place, the value, purpose and significance of the educational culture, and the knowledge of the people, already established in an educational institution. To do so ensures that plans for change are 'fit for purpose' in suggesting wholesale, or even partial adaptations to that culture. Since the knowledge, skills and abilities, attitudes and actions of people comprise the most significant resources possessed by any educational institution, changes are best imposed when these groups are consulted and their views are taken into account in the process.

Researchers such as Geus (1997) observe that, in business, the 'sense of community' is the most important thing in achieving long-standing organizational success. In working with the community of people that comprise an FE organization, department or classroom, this is even more the case. FE colleges are communities bound up intrinsically with the knowledge and culture of the people within them.

Achieving consensus, and building a new ethos engaging all the staff, is therefore perhaps the most useful aim we can have in carrying out change management. An implicit tradition of academic freedom in many further education colleges means that lecturers, administrators and other key staff have, by definition, different views and methodologies appropriate to their subject area, personal style or mission. Complex, specialist practitioner expertise is based around this, often built up over many years. A functional requirement to achieve diversity in professional, specialist ways is often an intrinsic part of the job of being a successful member of staff in many different areas of FE. These areas include staff who are managers, lecturers, technicians, learning resources staff, crèche workers, personnel staff, and many other specialist groups. If we do not respect these specialist areas of expertise in the body of staff, and acknowledge and build on such strengths when planning changes, we can sometimes lose more than we gain through change.

Achieving consensual management practices through the seventh 'e'

In conceptualizing whole-institution developmental imperatives on further education colleges over the past several years, we could identify that the three 'e's routinely required in business of *efficiency, effectiveness* and *economy* have been systematically demanded of FE institutions for some years now. Increasingly colleges have met harder and more specific targets in these areas, including the recruitment and retention of learners at every level. We could identify that a fourth institutional 'e' in *equal opportunities* has also been a strong requirement more systematically addressed over the past several years. A fifth 'e' could be identified in *e-learning*, for which specialist improvements in information learning technology (ILT) have been a focus of major national developments since around 1997. The sixth 'e', perhaps one of the most vital of all for FE, of *excellence in learning and quality processes* has been a major focus of inspection regimes, and, again, has been increasingly achieved more effectively in post-compulsory education over the past decade.

However, a seventh 'e', ethos, is, by contrast, mentioned less but sometimes assumed far more in further education institutions. Before planned changes affecting staff are introduced, we need to research the views of existing staff, to find out what they feel and think, and to recognize the hard truth that sometimes, no matter how hard an FE institution has tried to support staff through various initiatives, the generally cash-strapped nature of FE means that staff often feel very undervalued and overworked.

In recognizing this we then need to link action to our reflections, so that staff can observe not only that they are listened to, but that their views are significant enough either to change the plans of those planning change, or at least to be perceived as important in the process of planning changes. The results from this can then be used in a process of gradually and carefully introduced changes that will be supported by staff.

Building our capacity to identify and evaluate change processes

The implementation of practitioner research, carried out to inform and improve processes of change, can be invaluable for organizational improvement and growth. Staff delivering changes can be aided by in-house research planned and carried out effectively. Practitioners wanting to influence change practices can provide helpful insights to organizational managers, by making more explicit the deep-seated 'tacit' knowledge or 'know-how' about how the organization work's. This is particularly the case if, for example, the research process enables practitioners to feedback their views in positive ways.

In classroom practitioner research, the introduction of new teaching methods can be informed by 'critical conversations' with both colleagues and learners. Targeted research, focusing on limited, clear objectives – e.g. interviewing learners about their learning styles, and conducting a 'learning styles' (Kolb, 1984) test in a mutually rewarding educational development session – can lead to clear, informative results to inform the introduction of planned changes.

What skills and qualities can help this process?

Skills of leadership, objectivity, procedural rigour and good strategic planning are necessary to our research. Qualities of determination and enthusiasm are also necessary. Monitoring and evaluation skills, effective communication, consensual techniques for enlisting others' support/opinions, and empathic understanding of participants' needs are important. Awareness of and respect for ethical sensitivities is vital to the research. Perhaps, above all, coping tactics, including humour and relaxation, can help us.

The seven principles

We now suggest a way forward for busy FE practitioners when faced with implementing or participating in change. A simple seven step guide for carrying out effective action research in researching the management of change is suggested.

This is not a failsafe, perfect guide and it is not the only one. There are many change management works and research textbooks that will be invaluable to our work in carrying forward research into change processes in education. What is perhaps slightly unusual is the targeted nature of this short summary work, because it is written with the staff in the post-compulsory sector in mind, particularly those faced with the practical difficulties encountered every day by practitioner researchers in further education.

We have drawn together seven basic underlying principles that are fundamental to ensure the effectiveness of participative action research when considering changes in PCET/FE. These key principles must be present to some degree in carrying out any action research. Together they form a basic guide for carrying out action research effectively. They have been tailored to fit the environment of FE practitioner research.

These seven principles form the REFLECT model for small-scale reflective practitioner research for change management, as outlined in Table 2.1. We note each basic principle next to immediate action to be taken, and some related deeper considerations for the research. In the 'immediate action' column, we specify the different stages of *reflect–plan–act–observe–reflect* in the cyclical process appropriate to action research as noted by Zuber-Skerritt (1996) and Cohen *et al.* (2000).

These are placed alongside the *freeze–unfreeze–move–refreeze–revise* stages of forcefield analysis and change theory of Lewin (1952) as revised by Zuber-Skerritt (1996) and reported in Cohen *et al.* (2000). In the 'deeper implication' column, we elaborate on the immediate action to suggest a number of different ways in which the action research self-reflective spiral can be drawn out in practice.

In applying the seven principles, we note that there are three basic kinds of practitioner action research we can identify that are particularly relevant to changes carried out in post-compulsory education, particularly in FE:

technical changes;
practical curriculum changes;
organizational changes.

All of these can embody the basic principles of practitioner collaborative action research, but each of them has specific requirements and characteristics. We can define action research in relation to these areas in the following ways.

Action research for technical change

This kind of action research for change is typically limited to a specialist area of activity for a defined short-term purpose of improving an aspect of institutional effectiveness. An example would be researching the introduction of change to the management information system (MIS) in a college, or bringing in a new firm of caterers. Many colleges have carried out this form of limited, specific action research, perhaps using outside consultants to help, and advertising the results widely in the process of

Table 2.1 Seven principles in the REFLECT method of action research for change in FE

	Principle	Summary of immediate actions	Deeper research implication
1 R	**REFLECT, READ UP ON CHANGE AND ITS IMPACT** Reflexive informed selective contemplation on issues identified	**REFLECT – FREEZE** do selected reading, thinking and consult about ideas before changing anything!	Reflect about our practice deeply before starting; set up an action research (AR) group and consult with them
2 E	**ESTABLISH PURPOSE AND AUDIENCE** Establishing collaborative purpose and audience for research	**PLAN – UNFREEZE** Determine purpose and audience collaboratively	Work with AR group to critique practice and enable action for empowerment, making a long-term difference to practice through research
3 F	**FOCUS QUESTION, PLAN, MONITOR INTERVENTION** Focused planning and monitoring of intervention for empowerment	**PLAN – UNFREEZE** Focus the question on an area we can control and produce the plan for the action research	Clarify issue and develop a planned strategy targeting the research on a small area for maximum impact
4 L	**LEAD ON GETTING METHOD AND TIMING RIGHT** Leading the shared ownership of a precisely worked out research method and timescale	**ACT – MOVE** Get the method and timing right, take the lead and spread the vision in implementing research	Put the planned strategy into practice in a methodical timed way, leading the process and sharing the vision with AR group and others
5 E	**ENSURE ETHICAL AND POLITICAL SENSITIVITY** Ethical and political sensitivity in implementing data collection	**ACT – MOVE** Be sensitive to the ethics and politics of data collection during research	Ensure the subjects of action research are equal, respected members of community and observe truth, sincerity and ethics
6 C	**CRITIQUE REPORT AND DISSEMINATION** Critical practitioner writing and dissemination of findings	**OBSERVE – REFREEZE** Be critical about writing and disseminating findings of research	Critical and self-critical reflection in problem-solving should form part of the AR group critique of the report and its dissemination

Table 2.1 Continued

	Principle	Summary of immediate actions	Deeper research implication
7	T **TARGETED EVALUATION** Targeted evaluation of the impact of the research on change management practice and refinement of action	**REFLECT – REVISE** Evaluate by measuring the impact of overall change research in a targeted way; refine action according to the results of evaluation	The accountability of action research is tested in the evaluation and refinement process, with AR practitioner group involved in further discursive critique

implementing changes and evaluating them. Often relatively non-controversial, the action research process in technical change tends to involve people giving evaluative feedback about one particular system, organization or method compared against others. The quantitative and/or qualitative results are analysed and a decision is made, typically by a senior manager or committee, to introduce a new system or method.

Action research for practical curriculum change

This kind of action research for change is linked particularly with the idea of the 'reflective practitioner' in the classroom as outlined by Schön (1983). It is linked with the idea of 'situated learning' (Collins and Duguid, 1989) as it takes place in the teaching workplace, is grounded in teaching practice, and aims at improvements in learning and teaching. Reflection on action is linked to a cycle in implementing collaboratively agreed actions for change that are monitored and evaluated. Often focusing on a small area of operation, this kind of action research is particularly appropriate for teacher practitioners in further education.

Action research for organizational change

Organizational change can usefully involve a collaborative wider application of action research techniques. This application of action research has links with the concept of 'emancipatory action research' in challenging the operation of existing systems, hierarchical and social groups. It aims to understand and improve the operation of organizations and systems through introducing changes in democratic, participative ways. The work of Argyris and Schön (1974) on 'double-loop learning' that questions and challenges organizational value systems, Shön (1987) on 'reflection-in-action' and that of Zuber-Skerritt (1996) on action research for organizational change, are key texts here.

We will now explore each of the seven key principles in turn.

3

Principle One: Reflect, Read Up on Change Processes and the Impact of Research Before Changing Anything!

Whatever kind of changes we are contemplating, reflexive informed reading on selected issues will be very important at the outset. We need to inform ourselves about existing relevant literature relating to our research. Each of the three main areas of *technical, curriculum* and *organizational* action research for change has a field of expert literature that it is useful for us to consult. See Cohen *et al.* (2000) for an overview of this, or Habermas (1972) for more detailed further information on these three kinds of action research.

Specialist literature on researching technical changes

Since technical change research is typically limited to a particular, specified field of activity for a defined short-term purpose of improving effectiveness, we are likely to need to consult specialist technical sources of information. An example would be the researching the introduction of change to the information communications technology (ICT) system in a college, for which there are many specialist resources, user groups and publications. Many colleges have carried out this form of limited, specific action research, perhaps using outside consultants to help, and have sometimes published the results widely. See Cohen *et al.* (2000) and Grundy (1987) for further information on technical action research, and consult specialist FE sources of information: for example, the Learning Skills Development Agency (LSDA) website is a good place to start (www.lsda.org.uk).

Specialist research resources for practitioner teaching change

As this is the area for which participative action research as a small-scale critique of teaching practice is best known, there are many useful sources of information available. The practitioner teacher can implement planned processes of collaborative inquiry in a methodical and rigorous way. This can significantly improve practice in teaching and learning, empowering both teacher and classroom participants in the process. Through reflective practice we can intervene in action, observing, critically analysing and controlling changes for improvement in the classroom. See Cohen *et al.* (2000) for a useful overview; see Shön (1983) and Grundy (1987) for further more detailed information on 'reflective practice' in the classroom.

Specialist research resources for organizational change management

Organizational change aims to achieve wider institutional change than can be gained immediately in just one classroom or area of operations. It can still, however, be small-scale change, in the sense that it may be limited to one organization or one purpose. Many books and papers on change management can inform us here, as it has been the subject of keen theoretical debate for about forty years. Reading a small number of selected works can inform us about key theories on change management before we plan any changes. See Fullan on education change (1991) or Sadler (1996) on change management generally for key texts.

Some post-compulsory education managers have found to their cost that poorly informed and hastily executed changes can cause more trouble than they are worth. For us to know nothing at all authoritative about organizational change processes is not helpful. On the other hand, attempting to know too much too quickly, and getting lost in the vast theoretical jungle of change management articles is not going to help us either. It is not necessary to read more than a small number of key works in change management theory to carry out our research on planned changes effectively.

A large number of articles on change management focus on a 'how to' approach, aiming to promote successful change through one or other preferred methods. Such articles stress the difficulties of carrying out change processes successfully, noting that 70 per cent of all business change management projects fail (Beer and Nohria, 2000). Change management experts often categorize change methods according to three basic theories of change: *theories E, O* and *CEO.* While *theory E change* is based on *E*conomic value and 'hard' processes with a more ruthless approach, *theory O* stresses people-centred *O*rganizational capacity-building and 'soft' change processes such as building trust through teamwork. *Theory CEO* combines both E and O theories, blending 'hard' with 'soft' change methods. Balancing these two methods is regarded by some change management experts as the most useful approach to take (Beer and Nohria, 2000). Whichever theories we select for our research, it will be useful to read such basic guides to change management as Fullan (1991).

Change through adopting research and democratic problem-solving

Carrying out our planned changes in the three areas above by adopting actions based on the results of research is an authoritative and responsible way of planning innovations. Change should ideally be based on reliable and verifiable research results, not merely on theoretical hunches. Some people want to impose new operational models for personal or professional reasons not backed up by any real evidence of the need for change or the reliability of the methods to be adopted. Even when change is needed as a result of outside imperatives, such as new curricular, technical or funding models, it is important to plan implementation by carrying out an effective study of the conditions in which changes will be introduced.

Take time to reflect

Often post-compulsory education staff, especially those in further education, have little time to reflect on their practice as teachers, administrators, librarians, technicians or managers. We suggest even a series of brief spaces for collaborative reflection on practice, perhaps planned iteratively over a period of time, is invaluable. This can in the long run save much time and energy and contribute significantly to staff morale. We suggest those planning or expecting changes should *make time* for reflection both for individuals and groups as part of a plan for action research on improvement. This should be carried out before, during and after change. Even a few hours of staff development time planned for this over the year, especially for staff to meet in shared communities of practice, is a vital part of ensuring change goes down well.

4

Principle Two: Establish Purpose and Audience

Research must always have both an overall purpose and an audience in mind. Research without purpose is pointless. Purposes can vary, from the specific limited task of completing a thesis for a postgraduate degree, to the aim of fulfilling a government-directed educational initiative. The key point is that we need to be clear about our purpose, and to communicate the purpose and results of the research to others.

An audience for dissemination of the results of the research is also always necessary, whether this is, for example, only one person, like our supervisor for a degree, or many people in the wider community associated with a college. For further education practitioners at every level carrying out small-scale research, a selective audience may well be the most appropriate. This selective audience might be local, sometimes a key group of managers in an institution that is the focus of the research itself.

Purposes of research

The many purposes and audiences possible in further education research need to be considered when drawing up our research plans. Some basic questions we can think about in terms of purpose and audience for our research are the following.

What do we want to find out?
What do we want to prove or investigate?
What do we want to change?
How is this research going to make a difference?

If we have difficulty focusing the area of our investigation, and the main purpose of the research, testing our ideas with the action research group, or inviting proposals from them, would be a useful way of proceeding. To help us with this, there is also the following technique.

Create a metaphor to help decide the purpose of the research

It may be useful for us to think about finding a *metaphor* for the situation or entity we want to change (Morgan, 1993, 1997). The use of metaphors can be helpful to enable us establish our purpose, whether this is to solve a problem or identify best practice that needs to be spread more widely. Metaphors can translate the complexities of everyday situations into more understandable models. We can develop such metaphor to help us find insights into our work.

Metaphorical thinking can enable us to find radical new approaches that we have not yet envisaged at all, by freeing up our limitations in thinking. This kind of thinking can be linked fairly readily with the 'tacit knowledge' of the organization held by staff at every level but seldom expressed, and is often stimulated by visual metaphor. Metaphorical thinking can also be used at different levels – for example, it can help us to envisage an enriched learning environment that will help to achieve the best for both our learners and ourselves as teachers.

By carrying out an inquiry about the use of these methods, we can achieve measurable and specific improvements through research. Metaphorical thinking can also help us envisage what the worst results will be if we *don't* carry out any changes, or observe and inquire into the use of these at all.

Be practical about purposes

In examining and determining our purposes for research, we need to be practical about the possibilities. We need to examine whether our aims for the research are realistic, given time and money constraints and researcher capabilities. We need, for example, to be able to afford the time to do a survey, and carry out the analysis for this, and whether we have the skills ourselves to do it, or the resources to employ an expert to help us.

Be realistic about our audience

The audience needs to relate to the overall vision for our research. We need to envisage the intended recipients of the conclusions, to conceptualize the power they have to shape and use the research, and prepare for this. We also need to consider who else we are aiming at and why, including all participants in the research, and to guarantee that ethics and confidentiality for both participants and recipients are observed. In this, ensuring the dignity of the participants/receivers is vital, as is our consultation to get permission for the study. If the research is controversial for participants, the results of publishing it needs to be worth the risks (see also Principle Five). Our purpose in disseminating the results of our research, and its intended impact on the recipients can be critiqued in detail with the action research group (see also Principle Seven).

The tension between research aims of openness and truthfulness may sometimes conflict with aims to preserve the dignity of participants. The intention to ensure 'non-maleficence' (no harm) to any subject is a key principle that should be observed in all our research (see also Principle 5).

Practical example: an FE college principal using metaphor

A new principal is worried about the image of her/his college. It's a bit run-down, and seems like an old machine grinding away slowly, not very competitively, losing student numbers. He/she wants to reinvigorate it at every level. Deciding to choose a metaphor to free up the stale atmosphere, and create a new identity, he/she stimulates the staff to envisage the college as a fit, healthy organism. The principal holds a staff development day to discuss this and invites ideas from staff for the best new metaphor for the college as a living organism. Someone comes up with the concept that the college can renew itself perpetually and become like a water lily in a pond – a superbly fit organism with a healthy, networked self-perpetuating structure. He/she brainstorms this idea with staff. They become engaged in producing plans for a new organic structure based around the concept of the water lily. An attractive new college logo and image is created, and a new staffing structure collaboratively agreed and gradually implemented. There are both winners and losers in this process, but everyone agrees they enjoyed the 'brainstorming' and it was carried out well.

Practical example: an FE lecturer using metaphor

An FE lecturer uses metaphor to focus ideas of the classroom as a micro world. At present, it's a bit of a desert. The adult learners come into an empty cold classroom with no resources. Envisaging an enriched environment, the lecturer asks the group to help make the room more stimulating for learning. He/she asks them in a questionnaire for their views, holding a focus group with key participants. From feedback received, helped by the group and librarian, the environment is transformed permanently into a much more interesting space. It now has heating, carpeting, books, video resources, a comfortable seating area, coffee/tea facilities, and computing resources. The changes have in this case cost nothing but time, as the class has managed to get resources moved from other areas, donated, or lent to the group. They asked the caretaker simply to turn the heating on, got him/her to help lay down some new leftover carpet, and one Saturday the group all came in to paint the room, having obtained permission for this. The lecturer examines learners' use of the new areas through observation/ video-recording. He/she analyses the effect of these changes on learners' achievement results statistically, and interviews them to see if they feel the learning environment has improved. All indicate it's a 'richer' and better space to learn.

5

Principle Three: Focus Question, Plan and Monitor Intervention

Given the plethora of current new initiatives thrust on educational institutions, there is a strong need for us to find a focus for any planned changes. By setting purposeful limits, we can set our goals firmly on accomplishing worthwhile results. Establishing 'SMART' targets (specific, measurable, achievable, realistic and time-limited) is part of this, but we could also envisage our change project in terms that ensure we can be effective. Carrying out research to find this key focus for our own planned changes can be highly effective. In particular, the following are useful starters for achieving a realistic focus.

Use Gareth Morgan's 15 per cent approach to focus research to concentrated form

Gareth Morgan (1996) writes of the 15 per cent area of work over which most people have control and influence, 85 per cent being beyond our control, governed by forces far beyond our individual capability for influence. Morgan proposes people should concentrate on achieving good results in the 15 per cent of controllable influence they have:

> We live in a time when most of our organizations face the challenge of creating breakthroughs. The irony is that there is no magic wand, elixir or sure-fire plan to achieve this. The challenge rests in finding ways of creating transformational change incrementally: by encouraging people to mobilize small but significant '15-percent initiatives' that can snowball in their effects. When guided by a sense of shared vision, the process can tap into the self-organizing capacities of everyone involved.
>
> (Morgan, 1996)

Practical curriculum example: what can an FE lecturer control?

An example of a practical situation in which we could apply the 15 per cent focused approach could be for an FE lecturer teaching a poorly performing class on a Friday afternoon. The class regularly becomes rowdy and is underachieving. The lecturer decides to carry out research to discover what changes would be beneficial for learner concentration and better classroom and exam results. In this situation, the lecturer couldn't easily change everything about the time of the class, the college environment, the nature of the learners, their levels of prior education, the noise in the corridor, the heating, lighting or chairs in the room. But the lecturer could realistically carry out some effective research to examine the possible effects of changing the teaching methods and structure of the class to maximize learner learning (15 per cent). He/she could then implement this research, and once achieved, could adopt proactive new teaching methods to improve learning. To achieve success in planned change, research and action focused on the 15 per cent, can achieve unexpectedly large benefits. The basic point here is that the lecturer decides to focus on researching only those areas over which he/she has *control.*

This is somewhat different from the 80:20 rule that 20 per cent of effort achieves as much or more than the majority of the 80 per cent additional efforts that we regularly put into work. The 15 per cent approach is about focusing effort only on areas of influence that you have, and achieving results in these, rather than trying to tackle 100 per cent all the time. 'The 100-percent approach tends to spread itself too thinly, and actually mobilizes opposition to itself' (Morgan, 1996, www.imaginiz.com/provocative/solution.html). We can only achieve so much in life in the time we have available to us. This truism about our limited resources, time and energies needs to be translated into practical realities to control our change project, rather than the other way around. Some practical examples are useful here and are outlined in the boxed sections.

How to find your 15 per cent area of influence for small successful incremental change

Brainstorm the issues into a sketch identifying all main areas of activity.
Assign each area of potential influence to 85 per cent (no influence) and 15 per cent (have influence).
Select areas that are in the 15 per cent area of influence and list them separately.
Brainstorm the combinatory potential of aspects of influence (for example, I can control teaching methods, seating arrangements in the lesson, the nature of learner assignments).
Work out the 15 per cent area of influence that it will be useful to research.
Within this work out the question – e.g. will learners benefit from having this new method?
Develop a research design and method with 'fitness of purpose' to answer this question.

Setting goals for our research

Having worked out our 15 per cent area of influence, and our focused research question, it's now appropriate to set goals to achieve the research project. The iterative process of setting clear goals may be more complex than we think at first, but it is useful for us to clarify exactly what we want to achieve. Collaborative shared participation in goal setting will stimulate the motivation and enthusiasm of those who need to be productive in shaping and planning changes. We can't achieve all goals in the research project on our own. We need to realize that no-one will particularly want to work on goals that they have not been at all involved in setting, and involve colleagues as appropriate.

Practical organizational change example: what can an FE manager control?

An FE manager could apply a 15 per cent focused approach, for example to investigate problems with learner achievement. Let's say exam results have declined in about six departments for a variety of reasons. No-one can identify any that are immediately obvious. Learner retention has gone up, staff are qualified, work hard, and, in this instance, there are no external problems with exam boards. The manager decides he/she will give a detailed analysis of results against previous years to heads of department in a series of collaborative interviews to investigate and agree negotiated targets for improvement course-by-course. A report will go to the Academic Board in a year's time. By giving incentives agreed in a consensual, negotiated way with managers to investigate results and find solutions for themselves, he/she sets in motion an inquiry to stimulate all departments to improve. After a reasonable timescale, this will be publicly reported. It has influence, because all other departments will see the results of the investigation. Yet he/she focuses resources on stimulating the effectiveness of local department collaborative power, using the management structure of the college to maximum effect (15 per cent), rather than spending effort on a wholesale survey or a widespread punitive series of actions that may prove fruitless and arouse hostility (100 per cent).

6

Principle Four: Lead in Getting the Method and Timing Right

When considering changes, the importance of both method and timing can be crucial to our success. Leading the action research group to share the ownership of a precisely worked out research method and timescale is very important to ensure that our research project succeeds and reports in at the right time.

We have signalled the importance of leadership in this area because without it, the collaborative nature of practitioner action research could push and pull our project between different conflicting interests, and render it unworkable. The research project leader needs to resolve conflicting views in the action research group, and make sure that the project achieves an appropriate method and timescale to be effective. Setting, and sticking to, deadlines for comments from the group can be helpful here. Cunningham (1993) suggests the following, a useful pointer for PCET institutions, particularly those in FE that have little time and resources for carrying out lengthy research projects:

> The participative approach does not argue for months of field work and voluminous case studies as practiced by some social anthropologists. It suggests that much of the energy in a change process might be used in developing an idea and getting commitment.
>
> (Cunningham, 1993, p. 68)

Methods of data collection

Different methods of data collection for research on change are appropriate for different purposes. The methods of participative action research are particularly helpful to research small-scale change management in further education, but it's important to recognize that there are many other research methods that could also be considered.

In FE, an emphasis on short, collaborative time-limited achievable projects that have a clear focus to apply results directly to immediate problems, is appropriate. FE institutions normally have no additional funds to carry out research, are mostly over-stretched with existing commitments and we need to be realistic about this.

Having read up on the impact of change, determined our audience, and focused our research question, we need to select between different types of method for data collection to answer the research question in the most effective way. These could include the following:

interviews: informal conversational, standardized, open-ended or closed, group or individual interviews, recorded on tape and/or note-taking;
observations: structured observations, sampling of events, and/or naturalistic observation, recorded on tape and/or by note-taking and coding different events;
questionnaires: structured, semi-structured, and unstructured;
written accounts: commentaries from learners, including diaries and journals;
tests: standardized assessments of student and trainee learning, tailored assessments;
documentary analysis: of existing papers available on the research area of interest;

field notes, daily logbooks, journals of field visits.

More information on these different types of data collection is available in Cohen *et al.* (2000).

Keeping a research diary and maintaining a research database

Our research project must involve collecting and analysing a range of different data from the above methods. This data may include numerical and verbal information, and may comprise both original data and secondary data from published material. Whatever kinds of data we collect, we need to be methodical and meticulous in keeping notes on the progress of the research project, collating information and keeping research records that contain our data. Keeping a research diary is a good way to note down the progress of the project. We also need to set up a research database, to include all of the material from the project, organized in such a way that we can have ready access to different types of information within it. This can be kept in boxes and files, and we also may keep records on computer in an indexed format.

Selection of data for analysis

When we designed our research project and focused the question for analysis, we had already begun thinking about how we were to analyse the data. The selection of data for analysis needs to match the nature of the research question we are addressing, but in all cases we need to ensure that we simplify the process of analysis for ourselves.

In the use of *quantitative* data, for example, using an observation schedule that is set up to record events automatically could help us generate data through a computer-based data collection device. We can then import this computer file into the software programme we are using to analyse the data, generating charts and graphs for data analysis and report writing. The use of optical mark readers for questionnaires could also be selected, for example, so that the results of questionnaires can be generated automatically in a statistical data analysis programme such as SPSS. We can also manually enter data into a software analysis program if we are doing a small-scale enquiry that will not generate large amounts of data. We need to follow appropriate conventions on coding data that will be intelligible by others, for example organizing our data into rows and columns that are linked, for example to the records of observations or interviews we have taken.

In the use of *qualitative* data, our methods can be more specialist and more variable, but need to be no less rigorous, than in the analysis of quantitative data. If we have a large amount of qualitative data, the use of a computer to analyse it will be invaluable. Specialist qualitative data analysis programs such as NUD*IST are available that are essential for analysing, for example, different elements of language found in interviews, the meaning of different types of discourse, and patterns of regular and irregular word usage. Content analysis of different types of media, for example, of learners' journals, portfolios and web pages can also be carried out.

The analysis of qualitative data, in particular, is a complex area in which we may be aiming to search for deeper patterns of meaning from those available on the surface. Our project will benefit from doing particular investigation on the method of qualitative data collection and analysis to be used right at the outset. For example, if we are intending to do discourse analysis, there is a whole field of literature and a number of different specialist software programs available to help us in this area. The field of qualitative analysis is fraught with potential difficulties in terms of rigour and validity. We need to be both selective and specific in choosing which methods of data analysis to use, and how to plan the reporting of results.

See Cohen *et al.* (2000) for more detail on qualitative analysis.

Timescale planning and management of the research process

We need to develop the timescale of our research within the real-world context of our own classroom or institution, recognizing both the strengths and limitations of this. The timescale of the research plan should ideally be clearly outlined right at the beginning of the process, agreed with the research action group, and publicised. We should then attempt to stick to it, but allow for flexibility in the project to adapt to changes and incorporate difficulties and delays, for example relating to computer problems.

Mapping our draft schedule for the timescale realistically

In mapping our timescale for the research, we also need to realize our own strengths and weaknesses in meeting deadlines. We all have different demands, rhythms and family requirements operating in our lives. Sometimes unexpected crises occur from outside the project entirely! We need to schedule time to allow for some predictable interruptions.

This means that periods for work, reflection, rest, unexpected extras and, possibly, lengthy collaborative discussions, group analyses and feedback need to be incorporated within a realistic timescale for the project. We outline examples of potential timescales for each phase of an example research project in Tables 6.1–6.4. Using and disseminating a timescale drawn up with the aid of project planning software or even just a hand-

Table 6.1 Draft example timescale for AMBER pilot research project test for change.

AMBER pilot project testing	Wks	Calendar	Person responsible
1. Assess key issues of interest against organizational capabilities to carry out action research change management project	2	April–July	FW
2. Make time to reflect, read up, consult	2		FW
Select key informants/advisers	1		PS
Set up action research group and call meeting			
3. Build a theory-based plan			FW
Disseminate plan to action research group	2		PS
4. Evaluate changes previously carried out, check and modify plan against these	1		FW
Collate views of action research group			PS
5. Research staff/learner views, analyse results	3		FW
Disseminate results to action research group	1		PS
Final	1	April–July	FW + PS + action group
Decide to stop and modify research plan or go with the results of pilot	=14		

written schedule in a grid will be helpful to allow others to see when we intend to complete various parts of the research process. Running this past the action research group means that through public sharing and discussion, serious inadequacies in terms of practical feasibility should be revealed.

Our timescale should allocate time and flexibility for reflection and changes. It is helpful also to use a key expert in the subject who has carried out a similar project to help us check timescales for feasibility. Examples of different parts of the process are outlined in Tables 6.1–6.4, which consider in draft detail some real-life processes to make real the seven principles outlined in our model.

We have imagined this would be a small-scale project tested in the AMBER model in the summer term, in a process lasting around 14 weeks. A decision is then be made to go ahead with the main research phase, to last around a year, including the evaluation period. We suggest this kind of timescale might be feasible in a college operating on a 35–40 week teaching year. The timescale would allow for the results of the project potentially to be incorporated within the college by the following operational year. The timescale could be much more compacted than these examples suggest. We could plan a small research project that took only one term, or even just a few weeks. But in our model we are assuming we are researching an area that is problematic, complex and difficult, that would need time for reflection, adjustment and public debate.

We also assume here that the project would have a main leader (FW) who would be assisted by a senior project worker (PS), by the action research group (ARG) and a data analysis specialist (DA). The data analyst gives part-time limited expert help to the project, using

Table 6.2 Draft timescale for evaluation of small-scale research project for change: phase 1.

Main action research phase 1	Wks	Calendar	Person responsible
1. **Read, reflect, do literature review on change** establish leadership of project select key informants/advisers, consult them select action research group (ARG) consider ethical, political and practical issues consider data collection and analysis issues obtain permissions for project call together ARG + adviser hold 1st meeting and introduce project implement advice of group + adviser interview key staff re sensitivities of access hold 2nd meeting of ARG consider audience and reporting issues	6	Sept.–Oct.	Named members of the Action Research Group (ARG) led by the main Project Leader (FW), assisted by a senior project worker (PS) and a data analysis specialist (DA).
2. **Establish purpose and audience with group** formulate draft research question produce paper for ARG hold 3rd meeting of ARG incorporate views of group into plan			
feasibility study for data collection & analysis set up database for research data analyse feasibility study		Oct.–Nov.	

Table 6.2 Continued

Main action research phase 1	Wks	Calendar	Person responsible
3. Focus research question re-consider ethical and political issues produce draft theory-based research plan disseminate to action research group hold 4th meeting of action research group	6		Named members of the Action Research Group as above.
4. Lead discussion of plan inc. method/timing collate feedback responses from group incorporate into research plan			
5. Ensure all ethical/political sensitivities met hold 5th meeting: discuss ethics/ politics issues			
publish final plan and timescale	1	Dec	FW/PS
carry out data collection	5	Dec.–Jan.	FW
collate data			PS
End of Phase 1	**18**	**Sept.–Jan.**	

statistical software analysis and/or specialist qualitative analysis.

We could, however, carry out our project entirely ourselves much more simply, using just our own skills part-time, if we ensure to focus our question on an issue that can be managed through collection of our own data, using realistic and appropriate methods. Given this, our small-scale study in classroom or technical change can be just as valuable in its own way as a larger research project.

Table 6.3 Draft timescale main phase of small-scale research project for change: phase 2.

Main action research phase 2	**Wks**	**Calendar**	**Person responsible**
sort out database, classify and index select data sets for analysis carry out data analysis produce results of analysis scrutinize data analysis results triangulate different data sets write up draft research report disseminate 1st draft report to participants check for sensitivities confidentially disseminate 1st draft report to AR group hold 6th meeting of AR group	7	Feb.–Mar.	Named members of the Action Research Group (ARG) led by the main Project Leader (FW), assisted by a senior project worker (PS) and a data analysis specialist (DA).
6. Critique report and dissemination with ARG implement advice of group produce 2nd draft report disseminate 2nd draft report to all key parties set deadline for responses hold 7th meeting for final report discussions incorporate all feedback into final report write, critique and revise final report finalize dissemination schedule disseminate final report to participants disseminate final report to AR group hold final 2nd phase meeting with AR group launch report with ARG group, give thanks	5	Mar.–April	Named members of the Action Research Group as above.
End of phase 2	**12**	**Feb.–April**	

Table 6.4 Draft timescale for evaluation of small-scale research project for change: phase 3.

Main action research phase 3	Wks	Calendar	Person responsible
7. **Targeted plan for evaluation study**		May–July	Named members of the Action Research Group (ARG) led by the main Project Leader (FW), assisted by a senior project worker (PS) and a data analysis specialist (DA).
disseminate draft evaluation plan to AR group			
hold 1st evaluation meeting of AR group			
carry out evaluation study	5		
analyse evaluation results			
distribute draft evaluation study results			
hold 2nd evaluation meeting of AR group			
incorporate comments from AR group			
revise evaluation report			
publish and disseminate final evaluation report			
hold 3rd evaluation meeting to reflect on final impact and thank AR group for their work			
meetings with college staff on whole project	2		
plan implementation of results for next year			
End of phase 3	7	May–July	

Practical example: an IT FE manager carries out time-limited analysis

Governors ask the IT manager to report on computer usage, investigating whether the ICT system is popular with learners. Governors want to know this before allocating more funds. The IT manager uses a tracking system to monitor and analyse usage of computers at different times of day. This system identifies how often learners use networked computers and software programs. The results show clear preferences by learners for particular software. The IT manager interviews selected learners, also sending questionnaires to IT teachers. The results of the different data sets are collated and analysed, showing PCs are used intensively, but only with some applications software. The IT manager reports to Governors summarizing this and recommending purchase of more computers and selected software along the lines indicated by learner preferences. The Governing Body approves the new purchase.

Practical example: an FE assistant director using short-term research effectively

A college assistant director is concerned about the poor state of the canteen. He/she wants to improve it but has no money. The finance director says he/she will allocate resources if the assistant director can prove this is really needed. The assistant director compiles a questionnaire, distributing this to 2000 learners, asking for views on the canteen and whether learners would appreciate a new one. He/she has an excellent response: questionnaires are filled in during class time on-site. He/she analyses the results, discovering that 92 per cent of 1300 respondents say they'd like a new canteen and will use it. He/she writes a memo to the finance director cc Governing Body and Resources Committee, including questionnaire results, and proposing an allocation of resources. The request is agreed at the next Resources' Committee meeting. The research project is completed within three weeks, the canteen undergoes refurbishment lasting several months. An evaluation study carried out later indicates 87 per cent of respondents feel the new canteen is a major success.

Having examined the different options we need to focus on some key points of guidance. These are important regardless of the exact method of project organization we choose. These guiding points are that we are clear, purposeful and realistic in our timescale, and have both the meticulous planning skills and stamina to carry it out to successful completion.

7

Principle Five: Ensure Ethical and Political Considerations are Addressed in Data Collection

We need to be sensitive to the ethical and political considerations during the collection of data on change management processes. We need to recognize that this area is a minefield of complexity, varying enormously according to local circumstances, and that the issue of observing sensitivities carefully can potentially make or break our research project. We are probably all familiar with the horror stories of research carried out unethically, and the righteous anger in communities that can be provoked by this.

The image of researchers descending on vulnerable subjects like scientists in white coats with clip-boards and metal instruments of various kinds, to examine people in a mechanical, disinterested and exploitative way, is not an endearing one. Participative action research is very clearly a democratic collaborative process in which participants have an equal voice in the research process alongside the practitioner carrying out the research. We need to ensure, therefore, that our small-scale research process honours the values and principles of participative action research by establishing ethical and political appropriacy. This area will be particularly aided by the feedback arising from the participation of the action research group we discussed setting up under Principle One.

Ethics

The ethics of research is a complex subject that must be considered carefully in relation to the local situation of our small-scale research. In general, we need to treat participants with respect throughout the process, be sensitive and confidential about information that they give to us, and set up a democratic, open process in which all participants have an equal 'voice'.

Ethics is well handled in a number of specific works that are well worth the effort of reading. Cohen *et al.* (2000) devote a comprehensive chapter to the field of ethics, covering such issues as informed consent, access and acceptance, sources of tension, respecting the voices of experience, ethical dilemmas, ethics and teacher evaluation, and regulatory practices in research. Wisker (2001) provides a much shorter guide to ethics, appropriate for practitioners who are doing a post graduate degree. Blaxter *et al.* (1996) discuss ethics in terms of data collection and particularly with reference to gaining access to data.

In general, the following key issues need to be addressed in terms of ethics:

- confidentiality of data and participants;
- permissions to be obtained from all appropriate parties to do the research;
- access to be gained to participants and research settings in negotiated ways;
- professional attitudes to be upheld by all researcher participants throughout;
- moral issues to be observed in carrying out our data collection, for example making sure that no participant is harmed by the process, and that our data is truthfully collected;
- making sure that our participants give informed consent to the process of research;

ensuring that the views of our participants, fellow practitioner researchers and action research group are respected and valued, and they are appropriately acknowledged;
making sure we are carrying out a research project that intends to result in benefits to appropriate parties, such as the learners in the college or our learners in the classroom;
sensitivity to the concept of 'owing the data', which belongs to the project and the collaborative team, not to us personally on an individual basis;
making sure that participants have a 'voice' in contributing their ideas to the way in which the project is handled and the data is used and disseminated;
making sure that we are treating participants as equals in a democratic process;
making sure that we are respecting equal opportunities guidelines in recognizing gender, race, disability, age, sexual orientation, religious and cultural differences and embracing diversity and equality;
make sure the language we use in disseminating our research reports and written communications is inclusive and as clear as possible;
make sure we thank all parties and acknowledge them appropriately in the final report.

Politics

We need to be sensitive to political issues, with a small 'p' (for example, local college or neighbourhood issues about people's backgrounds, cultures, feelings and situations). We also need to be sensitive to any issues that emerge in relation to politics with a large 'P' (more significant political agendas, such as those to do with government, political party or local government issues).

Insensitivity to these issues in carrying out the research can cause our research programme significant problems, from limited failures and embarrassments within the project to a situation that could be a local disaster for our institution resulting in poor publicity if processes are handled badly. In general, action research for small-scale change projects seeks to work collaboratively and carefully with local situations. Our action research group should help in alerting us to significant problems with the way in which we are intending to carry out and/or disseminate our project. Among the things that we need to consider in the area of politics are the following:

- discuss the 'politics' of the project at an early stage with key informants, participants and with the action research group, to consider issues we need to observe about the local situation and the participants, for example tensions and rivalries between different factions to be researched;
- discuss any larger political issues that are currently affecting the area of work and its operations, for example, national or local government agendas, local LSC issues, local business or community issues that may be affected by the research process;
- obtain permission from and/or consult with key authorities when we have focused our research question and worked out our method and timescale, to ensure that they are consulted about key political issues;
- ensure our research project maintains professional objectivity as far as possible in carrying out data collection and in reporting results;
- be honest early on with key parties about what our project is intending to find, so that there should be no 'shocks' in the process;
- make sure that we acknowledge and thank all those who have given us permission and helped us on political issues.

8

Principle Six – Critique Report: Be Critical About Writing and Disseminating Findings

As we noted earlier, a key point about carrying out effective small-scale action research for change management in education is being part of a collaborative effort. It's helpful for us to share the process of critical reflection on writing and disseminating our research findings with others. This could be mainly the AR group we established earlier, but could also involve others, like key informants who are specialists in the area. Mindful of our audience for the research, we need to ensure that the items we discussed under Principle Two, *Establish purpose and audience,* are observed.

Schedule an open shared process of critical feedback for the report and dissemination

We should collaboratively agree an open process for writing and disseminating findings, giving appropriate deadlines, and sharing this information with the AR group. This process is best if agreed well in advance, and copies of the timetable distributed to members of the AR group and other interested parties, for amendment and comment if needed. It's almost always the case that some of the participants in our research have very busy lives and jobs. Therefore, if we want them to take an active part in the process, we need to be both organized about the suggested schedule and receptive to suggestions to modify it.

Once the schedule is agreed, the matter of giving and receiving feedback and carrying out dissemination becomes more easily manageable. Openly asking for feedback on our report and giving people a deadline to respond helps in the process of enabling us to be more objective and critical about both the report and dissemination process.

Using the feedback we receive to amend the report, it's good practice then to circulate the revised draft, with a final deadline to respond, before beginning the final publication and dissemination. It's generally useful to have some flexibility over deadlines here, allowing some 'cushioning' time in case deadlines slip, or key people forget to give feedback and need to be chased.

Receiving critical feedback on the report and dissemination process

Receiving feedback means listening to others provide communication about the effectiveness of our written report. To receive this in a useful way, we need to have a receptive attitude, stating why we want feedback. We also need to check that we have received critical feedback accurately, by repeating, paraphrasing or asking for clarification if there are obscure points. We should try to be objective about the feedback, and share our reactions to it if this is appropriate in the circumstances.

Effective feedback should be:

well-timed, specific, and requested, not imposed;
focused, constructively critical comments made about the report, not about the people;

empathetic as regards the needs of the report writer;
about writing which the reporter can control or change;
evaluative, not judgemental – sharing information rather than giving advice;
appropriate in terms of the amount of information the report writer can use;
checked to ensure clear communication.

Effective feedback can result in:

an improved report of the findings of research;
free and open information exchange in collaborative ownership of the report;
insight for both receivers and givers of feedback;
more effective communication and dissemination of research findings.

Group exercises to improve the effectiveness of critical feedback

To ensure that there is effective communication within the action research group, or the wider community of practice relating to our research, we could suggest some group exercises to improve trust and communication are carried out. By increasing the space for an open exchange of facts, opinions and feelings between the group in a professional way that harms no participant and establishes 'ground rules' for group behaviour, we can improve trust, quality and responsiveness to the real local situation.

Tact, diplomacy and protection of both the writer(s) and the action research group culture are sometimes necessary to ensure that a positive atmosphere of trust enables those writing and disseminating the research report to be ready and able to receive critical feedback. To encourage the writer(s) it is useful to employ appropriate positive responses. These should concentrate on an objective analysis of 'strengths' and 'areas for improvement' and ensure feedback is not taken in destructive ways that could be damaging personally. Group awareness and willingness can be built up over a period of time to ensure that the research process develops positively.

How to write best practice research reports of change management projects

In writing up the research on our change management project, best practice guidelines such as those advocated by Gough (2000) and Orna and Stevens (1995) suggest that we should from the first organize all our information in accordance with the structure we'll be using in the final report, by categorizing information into sections. This approach is easier for those naturally attuned to 'architectural' or 'bricklaying' and 'planner' writing styles, than for those naturally accustomed to 'oil-painting' or 'water-colour' methods used by 'discovery' writers, as identified by Chandler in his taxonomy of writing styles (Chandler, 1995). In other words, being naturally good at planning writing is useful for research! Even if planning does not come easily to us, it is particularly necessary for the effective organization of written research reports and, therefore, we'll need to adapt our preferences to encompass good planning. The following simple guide to help plan our report may help us if we follow it:

Devise a logical list of categories for our final report, for example as illustrated in Figure 8.1.

CONTENTS
Introduction
Background
Methodology
Data collection
Analysis
Findings
Conclusion
Bibliography

Figure 8.1 Suggested draft contents list.

Write a contents list of chapters for the report based on these categories, for example as illustrated in Table 8.1.

Break the chapters down into subsections, for example: Chapter 1, Sections 1, 2, 3, as illustrated in Table 8.2.

Place markers representing all aspects of our information for the report into the subsections, as illustrated in Table 8.2.

Mark out the key ideas throughout our report within these subsections.

Group these ideas together into themes, write up a separate list of themes, and number them.

In the list of contents, install the numbered themes in appropriate ways under each chapter.

Divide our list of contents/chapters containing the themes into boxes with extra space for more writing available in each one, and print out.

In the print-out of boxes containing our information, write out more fully the draft sections of each chapter of our report.

From this, compile the final framework for our report and start writing.

Table 8.1 Suggested draft list of chapters alongside contents listing.

Contents	
Introduction	Setting for research and for college, nature of subject to be researched, reason for research, for example to examine the reasons why urban young 16–18-year-old black females leave college in the first term, reference to previous studies
Background	Current educational trends, nature of subject area, local data from index of deprivation, local jobs available in IT
Methodology	Multiple case study: 25 urban-dwelling young black females in college studying IT
Data collection	Questionnaires, interviews and observation of learners in class carried out in July 2001, during 2 hrs a week teaching sessions for 20 weeks
Analysis	Data analysis: statistical, triangulating results of questionnaires and interviews
Findings	Publication of research findings in local college journal and LSDA college journal, discussion workshop at annual summer conference

Dissemination processes

A series of dissemination processes can be envisaged that will be useful for both wide readership and ownership of the report. In the first place, we can arrange for the draft report to be circulated widely to invite comments in a realistic timescale. We can then circulate copies of the comments received (if appropriate) and let everyone know that we are revising the report in such and such a way, as requested by various parties. If, however, there are

Table 8.2 Suggested draft of subsections within chapters alongside contents list for report.

Contents	
Chapter One 1. **Introduction** description of setting for college previous studies summarized nature of student group retention issues race equality issues prejudice and discrimination	Setting for research and for college, nature of subject to be researched, reason for research, for example, to examine the reasons why urban young 16–18-year-old black females sometimes leave college in the first term, reference to previous studies, brief discussion on race equality issues, nature of prejudice and discrimination
2. **Current educational trends** nature of subject area local data	Current educational trends, nature of subject area, local data from index of deprivation, local jobs available in IT
3. **Background** local situation of class 4. **Methodology described**	Multiple case study: 25 urban young black females in college studying IT, multiple sources of evidence from questionnaires, interviews, observations and documentary evidence
Chapter Two 6. **Data collection** description of method reporting of process	Description of questionnaires, interviews and observation of learners in class carried out in May 2001, during two-hours a week teaching sessions for 20 weeks in Brixton
Chapter Three 7. **Case studies of Helene, Chris and Jude** detailed in-depth individual case studies	Several in-depth case studies describing typical individual learners in detail

Table 8.2 Continued

Contents	
Chapter Four	
8. **Analysis** description of data analysis reporting of results of data analysis	Reporting of results in statistical tables Transcript of interviews Triangulation of research data
Chapter Five	
9. **Findings**	Reporting of overall findings
10. **Conclusion**	Conclusions summarizing key issues found Suggested further evaluation studies

important sensitivities surrounding this wide distribution owing to the nature of the data collected or the nature of the report, we may need to be a bit more circumspect about circulating the draft only to key participants first. This may include any identified party who is likely to have particular ownership or sensitivity about the report and the nature of the research carried out.

It is really worth observing these processes of shared public dissemination and ownership to ensure that the report is, in the long run, well received in the community in which the research took place. These sensitivities relate also to the ethical and political considerations we looked at in discussing Principle Five.

Having observed ethnical and political sensitivities, generally an open, wide dissemination of the report in a democratic way is an appropriate style of communication for the results of action research, as it is keenly rooted in the ownership of the group.

9

Principle Seven: Target Evaluation to Measure the Impact of Change Management Research

What is the overall impact of our study – methods to determine

The overall impact of our study can be measured in a number of different ways. These can be specific local outcomes tailored for and based on our study, or more widely applicable standard outcomes, or a mixture of both. The basic point is that we need to evaluate our action research and apply objectively recognizable methods to measure the results, so that we can analyse and report on the impact of the research in reliable ways.

What is evaluation?

To 'evaluate' means to 'judge or calculate the quality, importance, amount or value of' something (Procter, 1995). Evaluation is often an inherently subjective activity, as values can change over time and place, depending on the community of interested parties. Evaluating the worth and importance of educational research can be more complex and potentially subjective than estimating the value of, for example, physical objects, as research is so bound up with the perspectives assumed in and by different theoretical concepts. People may overestimate the impact of their research, thinking they have made contributions that are very useful to other people, when in fact others don't see this at all. How can we reliably determine what is of value in the impact of action research on change management? Who should be the judge of this, and how do we determine whether they are right or wrong?

Collaborative agreement on 'objectivity' of evaluation methods

In recognition that our subjective opinions may be flawed, we need to establish an agreed understanding of what 'objectivity' means in selecting evaluation methods for the research. Our research report needs to be open to objective scrutiny, to be truly responsible to the community of participants. But at the same time, we should acknowledge the complexity of such concepts of 'objectivity'. Some researchers argue convincingly that, since everything is subjective, there are no objective realities at all. Everything, in this view, could be reduced to personal opinion – in other words, if we think our research and its methods are useful, that's enough – they are! But such personal self-congratulatory research would be highly limited in its usefulness, lacking the rigour and diligence of being subjected to public scrutiny.

Validity and reliability

A self-congratulatory report that is valued only by ourselves would not be able to meet acceptable public standards in two very important tests for the usefulness of research – *validity* and *reliability*. If we want to achieve useful longer-term research results that can be replicated by others in an open process, we need to be conscientious about the role of the 'self' here, in the research process, and self-critical.

To meet the test of *internal validity*, we need to show that our explanation for the research data can be logically and accurately sustained by an examination of the data itself. We need to ensure the data are authentic, sound, coherent, credible, dependable and able to be audited by others, and that they have *content validity* in terms of being complete and appropriate for the research. To meet the test of *external validity*, we need to show that the research results are generalizable to other cases, situations and people, at least in terms of being able to be compared and transferred in general terms. To meet the test of *reliability*, we need to ensure the data collection process produces accurate, consistent, stable and replicable data over a period of time – for example in an interview situation, we can establish a formal set of questions that are used with all interviewees. Although it is hard to guarantee that all interviewees will interpret the questions in the same way, the training of interviewers and the use of inter-rater reliability tests in coding the transcripts may improve the degree of reliability. For more detail on the complex topics of validity and reliability in relation to both quantitative and qualitative research studies, see Cohen *et al.* (2000, pp. 105–33), who explore these concepts in depth, including a description of some eighteen different types of research validity.

Self-critical reflexivity

The concept of self-criticism as *reflexivity* – reflecting about our own thoughts – as an evaluatory tool to be used throughout the research process, is particularly important in action research. We benefit from developing practitioner self-conscious awareness and the rigour of our reflections during all stages in the process of the research, but perhaps particularly at the evaluative stage. The values, opinions, cultural attitudes and personal feelings of both ourselves and other practitioners and participants are inevitably bound up in the research process. The subjective elements involved are considerable. As participant-practitioners in the research process, we need to be critical when scrutinizing our own involvement in the research, agreeing collaboratively on the standards required for reliable objective measures to be used in evaluation procedures.

Tailoring evaluation methods to purpose and local circumstances

When working through our detailed research plan and its implementation, we also need to be sure that our evaluation methods are appropriate in terms of the purpose, audience, research question, timing, data collection and ethical issues as discussed earlier in Sections 3–8. There are many kinds of data we can use in carrying out action research, such as results from interviews, observations, surveys, questionnaires, case study notes, field notes, ratings scales, classroom journals, learner portfolios, audio/video recordings, and documentary records. A key point is to ensure our evaluation methods are locally specific and tailored to the kind of research question we are working on.

Educational evaluation methods

However, if we are to produce reliable, responsible, accurate and useful collaborative research that can be disseminated with confidence, we also need to acknowledge that we have responsibilities to try to ensure conscientious evaluation takes place. A general consensus exists on the use of shared, tested educational evaluation methods that seek to assess and explain the impact of specific interventions. These comprise a wide variety of different kinds of evaluation methods. However, in action research we are usually trying to measure the differences between the conditions that exist before an intervention, those that take place during the intervention, and those that exist after it.

For example, if a teacher is trying to work out whether a changed teaching method has improved class understanding, he/she might carry out a series of tests before, during and after the intervention. He/she might then compare and analyse the results of these with results from other teaching methods, to test the extent of the class's understanding of particular topics.

Continuous evaluation in small-scale collaborative participatory action research

One of the key points for action research carried out by reflective participants is that evaluation should be a *continuous* part of the process of the research, and not just carried out at the beginning and end of an intervention. Evaluation techniques should also aim to reliably measure results. The kinds of methods we can use in measurement are diverse, but these are the sorts of questions we can ask when deciding on the evaluation methods:

> What sort of effects are we expecting to test through our evaluation measurements? What do we seek to measure and how will we ensure these results are not due to chance rather than the variables we are measuring in the research?

Is the outcome of our evaluation generalizable to other circumstances longer term?

Are our findings from these evaluation measurements going to be relevant and reliable for our research and could they relate to policy making and resource allocation issues?

Evaluations can aim to determine the value of changes in learning situations. They could be quantitative assessments of the impact of teaching interventions on learners' results and attendance. They can also include cost–benefit or cost-effectiveness analyses, measurement of differences in organizational arrangements including staff, technical procedures and activities, services and facilities. Evaluation tools can include interviews with staff and learners, questionnaires, observations, tests, and a whole range of other measurement techniques. From the point of view of the research action group, what is most important is that our evaluation techniques and tools are appropriate to the research in question, can be effectively carried out, and that they pass required tests for validity and reliability. As long as these four basic criteria are met, there is some flexibility about which precise methods we adopt.

10

Conclusion

In these pages we have outlined some key ways to effect operational improvements in further education through researching change. We cautioned that major change is not always the best strategy for getting effective results from change management programmes, and that sometimes gradual renewal can be as or more effective. We outlined a number of key qualities and procedures that can help in planning small-scale change management action research, providing an AMBER action research change model for testing the feasibility of research at the pilot stage, and the decision whether to STOP and revise planned changes or to GO with them to the main phase of research.

We advised that there is a strong need to respect educational culture, academic freedom and the professionalism of practitioners at all levels in further education. We discussed consensual management practices in FE in terms of the seventh 'e' of *ethos*, in considering the importance of recognizing staff/learner values and culture in post-compulsory education. 'People-centred' collaborative research methods are sometimes both appropriate and efficient for educational research, and a focus on an iterative process of research in action means results can be applied within a short timescale, realistic for a sector with little time and funding for research.

Reflective practitioner action research has particular usefulness in building our capacity to identify and evaluate change processes in further education. From the critical and self-critical professional collaborative culture developed in a community of practice in PCET we can learn how to make improvements in practice and value existing strengths.

We focused on seven underlying action research principles in a REFLECT model, and identified these as fundamental to help us ensure the effectiveness of participative action research processes in post-compulsory education. These key principles for carrying out effective action research are relevant for FE practitioners at a number of levels in the organization of colleges, particularly in terms of technical, curriculum and managerial changes. Drawing from personal experience in the FE sector, and also from the literature of action research and change management, we outlined the following seven principles:

1. Reflect, read up on change and its impact, consult about ideas and plans before changing anything!
2. Establish the collaborative purpose and audience.
3. Focus the plan and monitor the intervention.
4. Lead collaboratively with precise methodology and timing.
5. Ensure ethical and political implementation sensitivities are observed.
6. Critique the report and dissemination.
7. Targeted evaluation and refinement of action.

We hope that staff in PCET more generally and further education in particular will be enabled to manage change more effectively with the help of these seven principles. Our goal is to contribute to the effectiveness of education for learners through good practice in collaborative practitioner action research. The uniquely supportive people-centred 'ethos' often already present in PCET and FE should be encouraged further. Valuing and developing the professionalism of staff and supporting the needs of students through reflective practice strongly benefits the sector. This applies not only to those who are the subjects of organizational changes, but also to those leading and managing technical, classroom and institutional changes. We have attempted to draw out these principles for conducting research to assist change management practices in post-compulsory education, relating these in particular to further education institutions. We hope that this will be of some benefit to FE practitioners in developing their capacity for action research for change, and will therefore contribute to the achievement of students in the sector, the main recipients of all our efforts.

References and Further Reading

Allen, D. K. and Fifield, N. (1999) 'Re-engineering change in higher education', *Information Research, An International Electronic Journal*, 4(3).

Argyris, M. and Schön, D. (1974) *Theory in Practice. Increasing Professional Effectiveness*, San Francisco: Jossey-Bass.

Bassey, M. (1999) *Case Study Research in Educational Settings*, Buckingham: Open University Press.

Beer, M. and Nohria, N. (eds) (2000) *Breaking the Code of Change*, Boston, MA: Harvard Business School Press.

Blaxter, L., Hughes, C. and Tight, M. (1996) *How to Research*, Buckingham: Open University Press.

Bloomer, M. and Hodkinson, P. (1997) *Moving into FE: the Voice of the Learner*, Further Education Development Agency (FEDA) Strategic Research Report, London: FEDA.

Burnaford, G., Fischer, J. and Hobson, D. (eds) (1996) *Teachers Doing Research: Practical Possibilities*, Mahwah, NJ: Lawrence Erlbaum Associates.

Chandler, D. (1995) *The Act of Writing*, Aberystwyth: University of Wales.

Cohen, L., Manion, L. and Morrison, K. (2000) *Research Methods in Education* (5th edn), London: RoutledgeFalmer.

Collins. J. S. and Duguid, P. (1989) 'Situated cognition and the culture of learning', *Educational Researcher*, 32, 32–42.

Cunningham, J. B. (1993) *Action Research and Organizational Development.* Westport, CT: Praeger Publishers.

Curtis, K. (1994) *From Management Goal Setting to Organizational Results: Transforming Strategies into Action,* Westport, CT: Quorum Books.

Elliot, J. (1991) *Action Research for Educational Change,* Buckingham: Open University Press.

Freire, P. (1993) *Voices of Change: Participatory Research in the United States and Canada,* Westport, CT: Bergin & Garvey.

Fullan, M. (1991) *The new meaning of education change,* London: Cassell.

Further Education National Training Organization (1999) *Standards for Teaching and Supporting Learning in Further Education in England and Wales,* London: FENTO.

Further Education Unit (1992) *A Basis for Credit,* Bristol: FEU.

Further Education Unit (1994) *Broadcasting and Further Education,* Bristol: FEU.

Geus, A. P. de (1997) *The Living Company: Growth, Learning and Longevity in Business,* Boston: Harvard Business School Press.

Gillham, B. (2000) *The Research Interview,* London: Continuum.

Glaser, B. G. and Strauss, A. L. (1967) *The Discovery of Grounded Theory: Strategies for Qualitative Research,* Chicago: Aldine Pub. Co.

Gough, C. (2000) 'Completing the research project', in D. Wilkinson (ed.) *The Researchers' Toolkit,* London: RoutledgeFalmer.

Grundy, S. (1987) *Curriculum: Product or Praxis,* Lewes: Falmer.

Habermas, J. (1972) *Knowledge and Human Interests* (trans. J. Shapiro), London: Heinemann.

Kemmis, S. and McTaggart, R. (eds) (1992) *The Action Research Planner* (3rd edn), Geelong, Victoria: Deakin University Press.

Kolb, D. (1984) *Experiential Learning: Experience as the Source of Learning and Development*, Englewood Cliffs NJ: Prentice Hall Inc.

Learning and Skills Research Centre (2002) *Research Strategy 2002–2005*, London: LSRC.

Lewin, K. (1948) *Resolving Social Conflicts*, New York: Harper.

Martinez, P. and Munday, F. (1998) *9,000 Voices: Student Persistence and Drop-out in Further Education*, Further Education Development Agency (FEDA) Widening Participation Report, London: FEDA.

Morgan, G. (1993, 1997) *Imaginization: New Mindsets for Seeing, Organizing and Managing*, Newbury Park and San Francisco, CA: Sage Publications, (1993) and Berrett-Koehler (1997).

Morgan, G. (1994) 'The 15% solution', *The Change Page of The Globe and Mail, The Globe and Mail*, 1 February, www.imaginiz.com/proactive/concept/solution/html

Morgan, G. (1996) *Finding your 15%: The Art of Mobilizing Small Changes to Create Large Effects*, Working Paper, Schulich School of Business.

Morris, A. (ed.) (2002) *From Idea to Impact: A Guide to the Research Process, Building Effective Research*, London: LSDA.

Organization for Economic Co-operation and Development (2000) *Where are the Resources for Lifelong Learning*, Paris: OECD.

Organization for Economic Co-operation and Development (2001) *Education Policy Analysis*, Paris: OECD.

Orna, E. and Stevens, G. (1995) *Managing Information for Research*, Buckingham. Open University Press.

Procter, P. (ed.) (1995) *Cambridge International Dictionary of English*, Cambridge: Cambridge University Press.

Robson, C. (1993) *Real World Research: A Resource for Social Scientists and Practitioner-Researchers* (2nd edition), Oxford: Blackwell.

RQA (2002) *RQA Quality Matters*, Newsletter of the RQA, London: LSDA.

Russell, B. (2001) 'Universities Miss Targets for Students by 40,000', *Independent*, 6 March.

Sadler, P. (1996) *Managing Change*, London: Kogan Page.

Schön D. A. (1983) *The Reflective Practitioner*, New York: Basic Books.

Schön, D. A. (1987) *Educating the Reflective Practitioner: Toward a New Design for Teaching and Learning in the Professions*, San Francisco: Josey-Bass Publishers.

Simons, H. (1996) 'The paradox of case study', *Cambridge Journal of Education*, 26(2), 225–40.

Stake, R. E. (1994) 'The case study method in social inquiry', in N. K. Denzin and Y. S. Lincoln (eds) *Handbook of Qualitative Research*, London: Sage, pp. 5–8.

Stenhouse, L. (1975) *An Introduction to Curriculum Research and Development*, London: Heinemann.

Wenger, E., McDermott, R. and Snyder, W. M. (2002) *Cultivating Communities of Practice: A Guide to Managing Knowledge* (Chapter 3, Seven principles for cultivating communities of practice, pp. 49–61), Boston MA: Harvard Business School Press.

Wisker, G. (2001) *The Postgraduate Research Handbook*, Basingstoke: Palgrave.

Yin, R. K. (1994) *Case Study Research: Design and Methods* (2nd edition), London: Sage Publications.

Zeichner, K. M. and Liston, D. P. (1996) *Reflective Teaching: An Introduction*, Mahwah, NJ: Lawrence Erlbaum Associates.

Zuber-Skerritt, O. (1996) 'Emancipatory action research for organisational change and management development', in O. Zuber-Skerritt (ed.) *New Directions in Action Research*. London: Falmer, pp. 83–105.

Index